MW00618385

"In *Seeing with Jesus*, Jack Glasgow practical but deeply spiritual guidanc individual study, you will learn to use develop your personal theological perspective based on Jesus. That perspective gives context to the thoughts and patterns that help determine even the moments of your life. The study of verses you may think you've known is surprisingly revealing. There is meat in every sentence, and you will want to read this more than once."

Jackie Baugh Moore
Vice President
Eula Mae and John Baugh Foundation
San Antonio, Texas

"What if we could see the world through the eyes of Jesus today? Jack Glasgow shows us how Jesus saw the world in his time so that we can train our vision to see and live into the reign of God in our time."

George Mason
Pastor, Wilshire Baptist Church
Dallas, Texas
Host of "Good God" Podcast

"Twenty-five years ago, I experienced firsthand Jack's giftedness for inviting others into community, into a space to learn, grow, and reflect. Since that time, Jack has remained a trusted mentor and a dear friend.

"In his book, Jack once again invites others into communion, a sacred, intimate space, to sit at the feet of Jesus and to see through Jesus' eyes the true kingdom of God. Here, we observe Jesus' teachings on the meaning of true discipleship, we hear his repeated call for us to love deeply, and we see through his eyes what is means to be a true follower of Jesus, modeling a sacrificial, giving, and servant love that comes only from God through Jesus himself.

"While living in a world that espouses a different view, Jack invites us to a transformative way of seeing and into moments of deep self-reflection on how we are truly living out a Jesus worldview."

Renée Lloyd Owen
Executive Director of Spiritual Health
Wellstar Health System
Atlanta, Ga.
Chair-elect, Good Faith Media

"Jack Glasgow is one of the most gifted and dedicated pastors I know. He has faithfully taught the Scriptures, preached the gospel and led Zebulon Baptist Church for over four decades. He is a cherished friend and colleague and a valued leader in our fellowship.

"Through this book the world will be blessed by his significant interpretive skill and insights. Jack reminds us that the starting point for understanding God is Jesus and the starting point for interpreting the sixty-six books of the Bible is the four gospels. I commend this book to preachers and teachers to guide their preparation as well as for individual and small group study.

"The questions at the end of each chapter encourage the reader to reflect deeply on vital questions about discipleship. For anyone seeking a clearer understanding of the Jesus worldview, Jack's guidance in this book is a tremendous gift."

Larry Hovis
Executive Coordinator
Cooperative Baptist Fellowship of North Carolina
Winston-Salem, N.C.

"You walk into the 'Vision Shop' in downtown Nazareth. They ask, 'How may we help you?' You say, 'I want to see the world the way Jesus sees the world.' They test your vision. It is blurry, indistinct, and dim. They write out a prescription. It says, 'Read this book ASAP. It will help you see the world the way Jesus sees the world.'"

Walter B. Shurden
Minister at Large
Mercer University
Macon, Ga.

SEEING
WITH
JESUS

**Developing a Worldview
Shaped by the Gospels**

JACK GLASGOW

© 2020

Published in the United States by Nurturing Faith Inc., Macon GA,
www.nurturingfaith.net.

Library of Congress Cataloging-in-Publication Data is available.

ISBN: 978-1-63528-108-8

All Scripture quotations are taken from The Holy Bible, New International Version.
Copyright @ 1973, 1978, 1984, 2011 by Biblica, Inc.

CONTENTS

ACKNOWLEDGMENTS

Nurturing Faith has been a trusted ministry partner through the years. The published journal has been an important piece for me personally and for the congregation I serve. It reports stories of interest to Baptists and the larger Christian community with a voice that sounds quite different from many of the media voices in our day and age.

Baptist congregations such as our Zebulon Baptist Church family near Raleigh, North Carolina, need voices that resonate with the moderate to progressive Christian community. I have often said that Nurturing Faith helps us to articulate the ethos of our church and its people. That is why I have been a loyal supporter and enthusiastic board member through the years.

I appreciate the confidence that John Pierce and Bruce Gourley of Nurturing Faith placed in me as they asked me to write a book for congregations and individual Christians to read and discuss on the worldview of Jesus. They have been at the forefront of encouraging Christians to question much of what we hear from political, social, and media voices that claim to represent a Christian worldview. So often the Christian positions strongly advocated by these voices sound nothing like the teachings of Jesus revealed in the Gospels. Both of these men could have done a marvelous job writing this very book. Countless other teachers and pastors have better scholarly credentials to address the discussion of the worldview of Jesus. But they expressed a belief that a long-time pastor with a passion for helping Christians to see the world through the eyes of Jesus could write this book.

I also express my personal thanks to the Eula Mae and John Baugh Foundation for supporting the publishing of this book. I have known the Baugh family through many years in Baptist life. Their commitment to keeping alive a moderate Baptist voice that can articulate a better way of following Jesus has been unwavering. I hope that my efforts in this work will be helpful in articulating this good way of following Christ.

Finally, I write this book at a time when I'm excited about the new day that comes with the creation of the new company, Good Faith Media. For more than three decades the Baptist Center for Ethics/Ethics Daily and Baptists Today/Nurturing Faith have served the Christian and Baptist communities by telling the truth to us and calling for the best from us. They have always encouraged us to see the world through the eyes of Jesus. Coming together as one media company, they are combining creative and passionate staff and merging their resources and strengths to keep a clear voice speaking to and for Baptists and the larger Christian community for years to come.

CHAPTER 1

Seeing from the Mountain

The gospel writer, Matthew, positions a discourse delivered from atop a mountain near the beginning of his work. We know this work as the Sermon on the Mount, found in chapters 5–7. In the preceding chapters Matthew has chronicled his telling of the story of the birth and genealogy of Jesus, including the visit of the magi. He has described the ministry of John the Baptist. He has shared with us the stories of Christ's wilderness experience, his subsequent encounter with the tempter, and his baptism at the river Jordan. The preaching and teaching ministries of Jesus commence in Galilee, and he calls the two sets of fishermen brothers to come and follow.

Large crowds are coming out to see and hear this preacher from Nazareth: "Now when Jesus saw the crowds, he went up on a mountainside and sat down. His disciples came to him, and he began to teach them" (Matt. 5:1-2). Over the next three chapters in Matthew we find sayings of Jesus not recorded in Mark, the presumed earliest of the four gospels. We find much of this material quoted in Luke's gospel, but scattered throughout the narratives, with the largest collection found in chapter 6. The setting is different: the address in Luke is delivered on level ground. Hence, commentators often refer to this discourse in Luke as the Sermon on the Plain. The material is clearly similar, but certainly not identical. The discourse in Luke is much shorter.

The Gospel of Matthew is known for its emphasis on the kingdom of God. The portrait Matthew crafts for us of Jesus is the one sent from God to announce and inaugurate the Kingdom. The Kingdom is at hand; it is here and now. Jesus announces the kingdom of God as a calling that beckons us to come and enter. All other earthly allegiances pale in comparison of importance with allegiance to God's kingdom. The vision Jesus clearly understands and articulates so well of the kingdom of God is at the center of his earthly ministry.

Thus, we see that Matthew has a clear goal in mind as he places the full discourse at the front of his gospel. He tells a story of one who has come to announce the arrival of God's kingdom and to extend an invitation to those willing to be subject to God's inbreaking rule. To talk about the worldview of

Jesus demands close attention to these beloved, sacred words that comprise the Sermon on the Mount.

A New View of Blessing

Jesus' preaching begins with the words we commonly refer to as the Beatitudes. The beginning of his sermon is quite unique and to the point: "Blessed are the poor in spirit, for theirs is the kingdom of heaven" (Matt. 5:3). Jesus goes on to declare that a condition of blessing is bestowed on those who mourn, the meek, those who hunger and thirst for righteousness, the merciful, the pure in heart, the peacemakers, and the persecuted. God blesses these with the gifts of comfort, inheriting the earth, filling and satisfaction, mercy, the promise to see God, being called the children of God, and receiving the kingdom of heaven.

This is a radical announcement of good news to those who at first glance seem to be struggling, downhearted, or oppressed. In the Gospel of Luke, Jesus makes an early visit to the synagogue of his hometown, Nazareth, on the Sabbath and reads these words from Isaiah: "The Spirit of the Lord is on me, because he has anointed me to proclaim good news to the poor. He has sent me to proclaim freedom for the prisoners, and recovery of sight for the blind, to set the oppressed free, to proclaim the year of the Lord's favor" (4:18-19). Jesus then tells the hometown crowd, "Today this scripture is fulfilled in your hearing" (v. 21). Luke casts the ministry of Jesus at its beginning as prioritizing good news for the hurting. Matthew does the same thing in the Beatitudes.

Like Luke, Matthew makes a clear statement about Jesus' ministry priority. Jesus announces good news of God's blessing to the down and out, the neglected and forgotten, the overlooked and the exploited. Wonderful gifts of blessing belong to these poor folks who would seldom come to mind when someone thinks of persons who are truly blessed.

How do we view God's blessing? Invariably we equate God's blessing with material things. At our Thanksgiving worship and family feasts we pause in gratitude for our many blessings: comfortable homes, plentiful food, meaningful jobs, good neighbors and friends, financial ease, physical health and the health of our families. Americans are often grateful for the blessings of freedom and liberty. We are grateful for the blessings afforded by our culture: economic and educational opportunities, recreational and travel possibilities, and personal and political liberties.

Left unspoken are the blessings of privilege we must surely recognize but seldom wish to admit. There are privileges of race and gender, of education and wealth, and of political and religious affiliations that give us great advantage over others. Many of us prefer to live in denial of these advantages; only a few are honest enough to admit them. But underlying these advantages is a belief that they are somehow, for some reason, God's way of blessing us.

We live in a culture where we are quick to identify the truly blessed ones as those who are successful, popular, powerful, famous, accomplished, and wealthy. The logical "other side of the coin" implies that the unsuccessful, the powerless, the little known, the struggling, and the poor must lack the blessing of God. We may not come out and say this, but we tend to either ignore or pity folks who seem to lack blessing. Jesus corrects our thinking.

The blessing of God is a persistent theme of the Old Testament. God blesses Abram and calls him to live in covenant with the Lord, with the promise of making Abram a great nation. His descendants will be as the stars, and his reward will be great. The blessing of God passes on through Abraham to Isaac and then Jacob. The blessing of God on the main characters of the Old Testament narratives is essential for their lives and ministries.

The priests of Israel are instructed to announce God's blessing on the people. "The Lord bless you and keep you, the Lord make his face shine on you and be gracious to you; the Lord turn his face toward you and give you peace" (Num. 6:24-26). These verses have helped me to articulate an understanding of blessing.

I see blessing as a gift of positive spiritual energy to another. God is shepherding the people. God's face lights up toward God's people. God bestows grace, a beautiful covenant love, on us. God turns a face toward us, regarding our lives with keen interest. God gives us peace, a full satisfaction with life, a deep *shalom*. To receive God's blessing is to receive the positive energy of God's Spirit. God is for us. God is with us. God loves us. God is at work on our behalf. God wants the very best for us.

For most of us when we ride through a neighborhood of elegant homes, we see the blessing of God. When we see a beautiful church campus with a thriving congregation, we see the blessing of God. We attribute the success of the talented and gifted to the blessing of God. Beauty, wealth, popularity, power, influence—these are blessings we see easily.

Then, Jesus corrects our seeing. He announces with bold and sudden clarity a whole new list of those who are blessed. We do not naturally view the poor and easily see the blessing of God at work on their behalf. We do not equate blessing with the grief-stricken, with the meek who may be gentle to a fault. We may appreciate or not the good work of the merciful, pure in heart and peacemakers, but we seldom identify the blessing of God at work in and through them.

Jesus sees what we have not yet seen. The positive energy of God is with these folks. The blessing of God is upon those whom many would overlook or pity. This is more than just a call to charity or missional engagement with the less fortunate. This is a whole new way of seeing the blessing of God. God is with and for these blessed ones. Can you see it?

Frank was nearing ninety years old. He was struggling with cancer. He had been a faithful companion and caregiver to his wife of many years who was dealing with memory loss that worsened over time. Frank had been a hard-working farmer through the years. As his pastor, I was there to provide some support through conversation. I was certainly sympathetic to the difficulty of his life situation and the challenges he faced as he was nearing the end of his life. Yet, Frank told me how fortunate he considered himself to be. He sincerely credited God's goodness as that which sustained him. This kind man said something I had never heard before but have never forgotten: "I am blessed, more blessed, and blessed again."

I love that phrase. When I heard it on a cold fall afternoon in Frank's den, I recognized in that moment the real truth to be found in the Beatitudes. It was a time of life where there was much for Frank to lament. Yet, he was sustained by the positive energy of God at work in his life. Frank was "blessed, more blessed, and blessed again." A few months later I would preach Frank's funeral service. His testimony of blessing moved his family and friends beyond any words I could say—blessed, more blessed, and blessed again.

Matthew's gospel speaks of Jesus seeing God's blessing on the multitudes. He calls them "the salt of the earth" and "the light of the world." Jesus believes they can do good works that will bring glory to God. Jesus lifts the neglected and downtrodden by convincing them of God's blessing and then calling them to a life of good works, ministry, and service. Can you see what Jesus sees?

A New View of the Law

In the next section of the Sermon on the Mount, Jesus offers a new vision of the Law. Jesus is quick to defend against charges that he has no regard for the Law and, in fact, states a clear intention to fulfill the Law and the Prophets. His mission is not to reject the Old Testament and its teachings. He is quite aware of the strong influence of pharisaic Judaism. Pharisees love the Law and stress its adherence. Their messianic hopes for Israel rest on a complete keeping of the Law. They have expanded the Law, building a fence around it with new requirements and practices, in the hopes of completely fulfilling the Law and thereby bringing God's blessing on Israel.

Jesus insists that the righteousness required in the kingdom of God must exceed that of the Pharisees. Systematically, Jesus introduces laws well known to his hearers by saying, "You have heard that it was said." Then, Jesus takes the well-known stated laws and adds new insight and understanding by saying, "but I tell you."

Jesus first talks about the law prohibiting murder. We recognize this as one of the Ten Commandments—one that most of us can say, with a sigh of relief, we have not violated. But Jesus takes this further by commanding us not to be angry against our sisters and brothers. We are to be careful to avoid hateful and angry speech. God does not desire to receive our offerings when we are at odds with someone; we must first reconcile and then return to the altar. We are to refrain from becoming legal adversaries with one another.

These words change things. A religious person can expect to keep the commandment prohibiting murder. But Jesus wants us to see the sin of our angry words and angry actions. The person who lives filled with anger and hatred, spewing contentious words that hurt and divide, becoming adversarial with others, is not living consistently with the worldview of Jesus. We can recognize murder as an act in opposition to the will of God, but can we see with Jesus the sin of our own lives regarding angry words and angry actions?

We have all heard the Law: we should not commit adultery. But what about lust? What about sexual behavior that treats another as an object, rather than a subject? In Jesus' day, adulterers were subject to death by stoning; persons were willing to destroy the body of one who violated the commandment. But who today is willing to mutilate themselves for their own unhealthy, offensive, and damaging sexual behavior?

Continuing with his new view of the Law, Jesus counters the easy out for men when it comes to giving their wives a certificate of divorce. Jesus offers a critique based on God's intention for the marital bond to be lifelong and thereby holds men as accountable as adulterers for divorcing their wives to marry another.

Jesus also talks about oaths and vows. While the Law has clear guidelines on how one must live up to the vows and oaths they make before the Lord and the people, Jesus suggests a wholly different course: make no vows at all. Resist swearing oaths. Simply let your word be trusted. Your "yes" means yes. Your "no" means no. It is the evil one, not God, who will lead you to go beyond your own trustworthiness to make public oaths and vows.

Jesus brings up the Law's instruction of "an eye for an eye and a tooth for a tooth." But Jesus says that we must have a righteousness that exceeds retribution. We are to turn the other cheek, give our coat along with our shirt, and walk the second mile when compelled.

The worldview of Jesus at this point is difficult for Christians to comprehend, much less live out. The idea of failing to resist an evil person sounds like bad advice. The meek and submissive act of turning the other cheek seems a bad strategy for dealing with abusers. The one who sues us for our shirt, does that person really deserve our coat as well? Does the Roman soldier who was free to compel anyone to carry a burden for a mile deserve our willingness to carry the burden an extra mile?

Yet, this is part of the teaching of Jesus. We certainly live in a culture more comfortable with "an eye for an eye" than with "turn the other cheek" or "go the second mile."

Somehow, there is a great strength that comes from hearing Jesus carefully here and in trying to follow these instructions. Jesus is teaching us that a mindset of retribution is unhelpful. Conflict only escalates when an "eye for an eye" justice is carried out. Turning the other cheek, voluntarily giving up the coat, and walking the second mile are not acts of weakness: they are acts of strength. There is powerful witness when these words are lived out.

The teachings of Jesus surely influenced the approach to activism of Gandhi and Martin Luther King Jr. The witness of the one who follows this counsel in the face of unjust treatment is powerful. (And, no one ever modeled this behavior more perfectly than Jesus at the time of his arrest, trial, mistreatment, and death.)

After his teaching against retribution, Jesus then speaks of radical, unmerited love. Whereas, the Law requires love of neighbors, Jesus carries the intent of God to a more radical place when he says, "But I tell you, love your enemies and pray for those who persecute you, that you may be children of your Father in heaven" (Matt. 5:44-45).

Jesus acknowledges that virtually everyone finds it easy to love those who love them. Even the despised tax collectors can match that level of righteousness. Most of us can greet our own kin and kind and extend hospitality—even despised pagans do that. Jesus calls us to love the hard-to-love, to love our enemies. Jesus calls us to act graciously toward those different from us, even those who may seem strange to us.

This sounds unthinkable: to love even our enemies. Yet, Jesus reminds us that such radical love, grace, and hospitality mirror the actions of God. God "causes his sun to rise on the evil and the good, and sends rain on the righteous and the unrighteous" (Matt. 5:45). This unmerited love and favor does not mean weakness. It is in keeping with the very character of God. For Jesus to ask this of his followers is a matter of encouraging us to act, think, and love like God. The bar is set high, at the goal of moral completion or perfection. The section concludes with Jesus saying, "Be perfect, therefore, as your heavenly Father is perfect" (v. 38).

Interpreting this section of the Sermon on the Mount leads to widely divergent conclusions. Some persons see the call to keeping the Law, far more diligently than even the Pharisees would have expected, impossible to fulfill. Some see Jesus as stripping away the moral pride of the Pharisees.

The Pharisees considered themselves to be keepers of the Law, and called others to follow their lead. But could even the most righteous Pharisee or the most morally obedient Israelite hear these words of Jesus and continue in prideful belief that they kept his moral admonitions completely? Who among us can hear Jesus teach us with his "But I say…" additions and believe ourselves to perfectly fulfill his view of what God really asks of us?

No matter how we interpret this section of the Sermon on the Mount, we must all acknowledge the unique vision Jesus brings to interpreting the Law. Righteousness is more than an external conformity to a legal standard;

it also involves the heart. It includes our motives. Jesus viewed the perfect keeping of the Law as much more than did anyone else in his day. His view of righteousness and law-keeping keeps us from prideful sanctimony, from exalting ourselves while condemning others. And yet, we are not excused from trying to keep the Law in spite of our inevitable failures in godly righteousness. We are still called to strive, to be perfect, even as God is perfect.

A New View of Religious Practices

We move to Matthew 6 where Jesus describes his view of how righteousness should be practiced. Religious piety is not an outward show to earn the respect of others. Practicing righteousness for the favor of others yields an earthly reward, but none from God. Piety genuinely practiced to please God is therefore done apart from showy, public display.

The needy should receive our gifts. But giving with public display is an act done by hypocrites. Gifts to relieve the suffering of the poor should be done quietly, where one does not "let your left hand know what the right hand is doing" (Matt. 6:4). Our prayers are not for impressing others in public with our many, pious words. Instead Jesus gives us a model for praying that we know as the Lord's Prayer.

The simplicity of the prayer is both its genius and its beauty. God is honored. God's kingdom is anticipated. We ask for daily bread to sustain us. We ask for forgiveness even as we recognize our need to extend forgiveness. We ask that we not be led into temptation and that we be delivered from evil. God's kingdom and its glory are recognized. The spiritual discipline of fasting is to be practiced with no show of how great the participant is sacrificing and suffering.

The issue of reward is at the heart of Christ's teaching. There are those who practice religious piety for outward show. Their charity, prayers, and fasts are attention-seeking devices to earn respect in religious circles. Their affirmation from others in response to their piety is their reward. Jesus is encouraging his hearers to practice faith, to engage in spiritual disciplines, for a much higher and nobler reason. Give, pray, and fast without regard to being seen and appreciated by others. Do these things and more out of devotion to God, and God will indeed give a gracious reward.

A New View of Material Things

Next, Jesus addresses the desire to store up large amounts of earthly treasure. In a world where tapestries and precious metals are indicative of great wealth, Jesus warns that these treasures can be victims of moths and rust. They are also enticing targets for thieves. Instead of desiring to store up these measures of earthly wealth, a person should seek to be rich toward God, storing up treasures in heaven.

Jesus warns us about following the inclination to seek everything our eyes see and desire. He speaks with simple clarity: "No one can serve two masters. You will either hate the one and love the other, or you will be devoted to the one and despise the other. You cannot serve both God and money" (Matt. 6:24). Persons in the church know these words and can recite them. But how many have allowed the worldview of Jesus to shape their own worldview at this point?

We live in a time when wealth increases with disproportionate distribution. The share of wealth accumulated by the wealthiest—the top one percent, five percent, or ten percent—is growing significantly in our time. Recent, sustained economic growth in our culture has increased the wealth of the bottom half of our population negligibly. But the increased wealth of the rich has been significant. Where are the warnings based on the teaching of Jesus?

Surely we can see that Jesus warns against the accumulation of great wealth and points out the incongruity of claiming to be a servant of God while expending great effort and energy to amass boundless wealth. The church seems willing to excuse the lust for increased wealth, especially if the wealthy will remember the church with contributions. But the pragmatic willingness of the church to court wealth does not change the fact that Jesus clearly warns us, "You cannot serve both God and money."

So much of the anxiety of life is tied to the concern for having enough. Will we have enough to eat? Will we have enough for our future? I have observed the changes toward wealth among Christians in the past thirty years, particularly as traditional retirement plans have been replaced by private investment accounts. No longer promised a guaranteed retirement income that is a significant portion of one's salary at the time of retirement, we are encouraged to set aside enough to last us through retirement and to provide something for our heirs. Our churches are filled with members, including clergy, anxious to know if their half million, one million, or even two million dollars of accumulated investments will be enough to sustain their standard of living throughout their lives.

So, while people are starving in parts of the world, hungry and/or homeless in our own towns and cities, denied good food, clean water, basic health care, and a safe place to live, we are worried that our 401Ks are just not robust enough to take care of us. Financial anxiety and worry occupy our thoughts and discourage our generosity as stewards. At what point will we admit that we are living in contradiction to the worldview of Jesus?

Jesus simply tells us not to worry about these things. Life is about something bigger than the concern for material things. Look at the birds and the flowers. They find what they need to survive. God takes care of them. God provides what is needed for what God has created. Trust this. "So, do not worry saying, 'What shall we eat?' or 'What shall we drink?' or 'What shall we wear?' For the pagans run after all these things, and your heavenly Father knows that you need them. But seek first his kingdom and his righteousness, and all these things will be given to you as well. Therefore, do not worry about tomorrow, for tomorrow will worry about itself. Each day has enough trouble of its own" (Matt. 6:31-34).

At some point, honesty requires us to admit how difficult it is for persons who claim to follow Jesus but who live in a culture that exalts wealth and the security that wealth provides to adopt the worldview of Jesus related to material wealth. Our shame is that we have refused to even recognize the cognitive dissonance between how we think about and see things and how Jesus viewed things. Yet, in recognizing how the wealth we accumulate never seems to be enough and that our anxiety over our future only seems to worsen in spite of our increased accumulation of wealth, surely we can see that the worldview of Jesus is worth investigating. Seldom do our financial advisors deliver on their promise of freeing us from anxiety about our future. Perhaps it is time to consider if seeing more like Jesus sees might be our best strategy of freeing ourselves from paralyzing anxiety about the future.

A New View of Judgment

"Do not judge, or you too will be judged" (Matt. 7:1). I recently commented to a small group that I felt Jesus was clear about refraining from rendering moral judgments of others. I went on to say that I do not believe the world needs the moral pronouncements of Christians. Instead, the world needs our proclamation of God's love in Christ and the incarnation of that love, demonstrated by good works we do in the name of Jesus.

When I said this, you would have thought I had three eyes by the incredulous looks I received. I interpreted the reactions of my hearers as saying, "Of course the world needs the church to stand strong with its moral judgments. Certainly we must be clear on what is right and wrong. People really need us to be clear about their behaviors that are inconsistent with the will of God. Jesus needs the church to practice and proclaim its moral judgment." I get their reasoning and appreciate why it seems valid. The only problem is, Jesus tells us plainly: "Do not judge."

Jesus knew the tendency of righteous folks to gouge into the eyes of others to remove the specks found in their eyes, ignoring the beams in their own eyes. Jesus viewed the hypocrisy of the self-righteous clearly. They were all too willing to judge sinners while blind to their own sin.

In our day we love to say, "Love the sinner, but hate the sin." But I think we need to admit that few people hear Christians say this about some behavior of theirs that we judge to be sinful and still feel loved by us. Invariably we say this about a few things that we are absolutely confident are sinful—ignoring that there may be real questions about our certainty of what is and is not sinful. We judge these behaviors while failing to acknowledge the blind spots in ourselves, the sins we excuse or cover or simply decide are not the "big sins" that need public discourse.

I believe Jesus intentionally placed the prohibition regarding judging others immediately after his teaching on wealth, on putting God's kingdom and righteousness above everything else, and freeing ourselves from worry over the future and anxiety over amassing riches. Be honest about something you consider a sin that you are quick to point out. Think about some behavior that you simply believe God is clear to condemn and therefore you are prone to judge. Then, think about how well you have followed the teaching of Jesus in the preceding section of this great sermon. Are you removing the speck in another's eye in spite of the beam in your own? Are you willing to follow the teaching of Jesus, "Do not judge"?

Jesus follows this teaching about judging others with a strange saying: "Do not give dogs what is sacred; do not throw your pearls to pigs. If you do, they may trample them under their feet, and tear you to pieces" (Matt. 7:6). I have never really understood this saying. I know I can read commentaries for insight. Jews would certainly not have been unwilling to label Gentiles "dogs" and "pigs."

Jesus is clearly critiquing the hypocrites of his day and age. He has used the term repeatedly to contrast his worldview from their belief and practice. Perhaps it is the religious, self-righteous keepers of laws and customs who are quick to judge what they perceive as irreligious and sinful that may be the real "dogs" and "pigs." They are certainly the ones who cannot fathom a faith that relinquishes the right to judge others. They cannot endorse a religious worldview that fails to label and identify the sinners apart from the righteous. And, experience shows us that these righteous judges will be the first to "tear apart" anyone who suggests that the followers of Jesus have been taught to refrain from judging others.

Test my theory. When you hear Christians pronouncing their moral judgments of a particular sin, gently remind them that Jesus asked us to refrain from judging others. You just may see what Jesus meant by the dogs and pigs who will tear you to pieces. There is a long history of wounded Christians who dared to suggest that followers of Jesus should refrain from judgment.

A New View of Knowledge

In Matthew 7, Jesus encourages a pursuit of truthful knowledge: "Ask and it will be given to you; seek and you will find; knock and the door will be opened to you. For everyone who asks receives; the one who seeks finds; and to the one who knocks, the door will be opened" (vv. 7-8). Some commentators point out an understanding of these verbs to indicate persistent asking, seeking, and knocking. But the promise is the result of our quest.

God is not hiding truth from us. We are not beholden to an enlightened few to discern spiritual truth. Jesus employs a logical way of viewing God. If we trust ourselves to know how to give good and appropriate gifts to our children, then how much more should we trust God to give us what we need?

There is a narrow gate that beckons our entrance into the kingdom of God and the true life it affords. These incredible teachings of Jesus represent for me the narrow gate. As clear and powerful as the discourse in the Sermon on the Mount is, I marvel at how seldom it has been truly embraced and followed by the supposed disciples of Jesus. It seems that only a few are willing to try and see the world as Jesus sees it. We are unwilling to fit ourselves through what looks like such a narrow gate to adopt a Jesus way of viewing blessing, righteousness, religious practice, living without anxiety over material things, and relinquishing our right to judge others. The broader gate that more will enter continues to view things as did the Pharisees—the hypocrites—and less like Jesus. But Jesus is clear. The narrow gate he opens for us with these amazing teachings leads to life.

The wider gate and broader road have been taken by more Christians throughout the history of the church and is certainly the more popular path taken in our culture today. We appreciate the hymnic beauty of the Beatitudes and appreciate the exposition of the Law. We know that Jesus warns against practicing piety for the attention of others, and are aware of the warnings against materialism and the invitation to an anxious-free life when it comes to having what we need to live. We can quote "seek ye first" and make it into a nice chorus. We will admit we have been warned against judging. We like the promises with regard to our asking, seeking, and knocking. But have we entered the narrow door that leads to life, the narrow door that asks us to adopt this Jesus way of thinking and living? No, the larger response has been to keep viewing the world through the lenses of culture and cultural religion. But Jesus warns us: This path leads to destruction.

In my lifetime I have been taught that this contrast regarding the narrow gate and the wider gate and broader road refers to our salvation, or more exactly, to our eternal destiny. But I see this as Jesus speaking to his would-be followers. This is less about our eternal destiny and more about our witness in the here and now. The teachings of Jesus in the Sermon on the Mount define the narrow path. To adopt these teachings and live by them is the way to abundant life. These views articulated by Jesus should be the views of the church. This is how we then should live.

Jesus warned that there would be false teachers. Be careful. You will know them by their fruits. They will plead their case that they have led many for the Lord's sake, done great things in God's name. But Jesus will be clear in his judgment of their false discipleship. We can point to many who claim the name of Jesus for their ministry. They may draw large crowds and impact many lives. They may bear the marks of success, but do they view the world anything like Jesus?

At what point do we hear them encourage others to accept the teachings of this amazing sermon? In what ways do we see them living by these teachings, walking in the narrow way? How do they view blessing? How do they view righteousness? How do they practice their faith? What do they demonstrate with regard to material wealth and possessions? Do they heed the admonition against judging others?

Yes, by their fruits you can tell who walks through the wider gate and on the broader path. Few are the true practitioners of the narrow way, who live with a worldview set forth by Jesus. Seldom will these few rise to prominence. But they are walking the path that leads to life.

And so, we must decide: Will we heed the words of Jesus set forth in the Sermon on the Mount? Will we build the very foundation of our lives on his teaching? Will our churches adopt living in the narrow way of these amazing words of Jesus?

Our decision matters greatly. The storms of life will surely come and challenge us. What we build on these words will stand the test of time. Living with the worldview of Jesus will keep us standing, as individual followers of Jesus and as communities of faith. Failure to adopt the views of Jesus, to live by his words may not cost much in the short run. We may be successful, and our congregations may appear successful. But when the storms come, the broader worldview of culture proves to be a poor foundation. The broad way leads to destruction, but the narrow way leads to life. No sermon ever ended with a clearer call to decide.

Questions for Discussion/Reflection

1. Try to recall how you may have articulated your gratitude for your blessings this past Thanksgiving. What did you name as your blessings? Now, after a careful look at how Jesus spoke of blessing at the beginning of the Sermon on the Mount, how do you think you might restate your true blessings from God? How willing are persons in our culture to see the persons named among the blessed by Jesus as the truly blessed of God?

2. Play a game of "before and after." First, before reading the words of Jesus regarding his interpretation of the Law in the Sermon on the Mount, if someone asked you, "How well do you keep God's laws and commandments?" what would you say? Now, after reading the words of Jesus in the "You have heard that it was said, but I say" section of the sermon, how does your answer to the same question change? What point do you believe Jesus is trying to make for his hearers through these new ways to view the various laws? Do you see this as a critique of self-righteousness?

3. Jesus taught the need for privacy and humility in the practices of almsgiving, prayer, and fasting. How do you reconcile the communal aspect of coming together for worship and spiritual formation with the call for practicing these disciplines "in secret"? What reward in heaven do you think Jesus was encouraging us to pursue versus receiving our reward through the affirmation of those who see and commend our piety?

4. How are teachings on abstaining from worry over material things received today? Do we take this seriously at all? In congregations filled with persons following the financial counsel of advisors who encourage 401Ks and savings to total between one and two million dollars in order to make it happily through retirement, what defense can you make that we take these words of Jesus with any seriousness? Given that few of us know Christians who "give no thought for the morrow," including ourselves, do these words of Jesus matter to us at all?

5. How seriously are you willing to take the clear admonition against judging others? Are you willing to finally heed the teaching of Jesus and relinquish the role of standing as moral judge of others?

6. Who are your best examples of persons who have embraced the teachings of Jesus in the Sermon on the Mount with seriousness? How do their lives look? How strange do those who live according to these words seem in our culture? Do you really believe that to embrace and follow these teachings of Jesus builds the best foundation for life?

CHAPTER 2

Seeing with His Disciples

Jesus chose to call persons to come and follow. The sets of fishermen brothers were early followers: James and John, Andrew and Peter. Matthew left the life of a tax collector. Eventually Jesus named a group of twelve. They were not his only followers, however.

Scriptures teach us of the devotion and benevolent support of women who followed Jesus. We are told of a sending-out of seventy (or seventy-two, as some translations report), paired with partners to go and do the work of ministry. But there were twelve called to be part of a special group of learners.

The Twelve were to learn from Jesus by watching, by listening, by seeing a whole new way of living, by being transformed into the likeness of their teacher. The called disciples grew into the role of the apostles of the early church. Their exemplary courage and passionate devotion to their Lord helped the disciples to lead extraordinary lives.

The Call to Follow

Christians use varied language to describe their commitment to Jesus. I grew up in an evangelical culture and in a Baptist congregation where the emphasis was on the act of "accepting Jesus as Lord and Savior." Describing the moment one received salvation could also be described with statemens such as these:

- "I gave my life to Jesus."
- "I asked Jesus to come into my heart."
- "I got saved." (apologies to our grammar teachers)
- "I professed my faith."
- "I walked the aisle."
- "I joined the church."
- "I trusted Christ as my Savior."
- "I expressed my belief in the gospel."
- "I was led to Christ by believing what someone shared with me about Jesus." (perhaps the Romans Road or the Four Spiritual Laws)

- "I prayed the prayer of salvation."
- "I trusted Jesus."
- "I confessed my sins."
- "I got baptized."

Our words indicating our understanding of what it meant to be a Christian were quite propositional and transactional. We viewed salvation as focused on a singular moment in time, a particular assent to the story of the death, burial, and resurrection of Christ. In my Baptist context one was "lost" until that moment came to be realized. But once one acknowledged personal belief through a prayer or public profession or baptism, then one's salvation was eternally secure.

What this understanding misses is seeing discipleship the way Jesus saw it. For Jesus, the call was always "Follow me." Of course, following always requires an initial willingness. The journey of following requires a first step. But while the church has often defined Christian faith as an act of profession, or confirmation that essentially assures one of salvation, Jesus preferred to call persons to come and follow.

Discipleship is lived out through a journey of following—a following that calls for listening and learning and for service and sacrifice. Nothing in the Gospels indicates Jesus ever reduced the life he wanted for those whom he called to simply involve a one-time event of assenting to propositions or making up public professions, or demonstrating outward ritual.

"'Come follow me,' Jesus said, 'and I will send you out to fish for people.' At once they left their nets and followed him" (Matt. 4:19-20). The journeys of Andrew and Peter, James and John were underway. Their lives would never be the same. Following required a commitment that lasted for a lifetime.

"As Jesus went on from there, he saw a man sitting at the tax collector's booth. 'Follow me,' he told him, and Matthew got up and followed him" (Matt. 9:9). Life changed radically for Matthew. The well-off but outcast tax gatherer was now welcomed into the circle of disciples.

The disciples showed a remarkable willingness to leave behind the lives they knew for the novel life of following Jesus. In a conversation following the encounter with the one we often refer to as the rich, young ruler, Peter says to Jesus, "We have left everything to follow you! What then will there be for us?" (Matt. 19:27). Jesus replies:

Truly I tell you, at the renewal of all things, when the Son of Man sits on his glorious throne, you who have followed me will also sit on twelve thrones, judging the twelve tribes of Israel. And everyone who has left houses or brothers or sisters or father or mother or wife or children or fields for my sake will receive a hundred times as much and will inherit eternal life. But many who are first will be last, and many who are last will be first. (Matt. 19:28-30)

In my own spiritual journey as a pastor I have felt increasing clarity in seeing the Christian life as first and foremost a call to follow Jesus. The language that speaks of salvation as a transaction, an assent to propositional truth, rings hollow over time. The grace and faith which is the gift of God that saves is rooted in a call to trust Jesus and heed his call to follow. This transition in my own thinking is rooted in more honest and open reading of the Scriptures. The language Jesus used with his disciples called persons to a lifetime journey of following. Whatever sacrifices they made—or that we make—pale in comparison to the blessings received on this journey of faith.

The Cost of Discipleship

How easy we sometimes want to make the whole notion of the Christian life! Just believe the right things, pray the right prayer, confess personal faith, be baptized into the church—and everything is taken care of for eternity. I am not arguing against the importance of doing any of these things, but I do believe we often fail to see the life of faith as Jesus saw it and as he taught his disciples.

Close to the midpoint of Mark's gospel the fame of Jesus is growing. The amazing and miraculous signs he has performed, coupled with the intriguing teachings unlike any heard before, have led to increased notoriety for Jesus and his followers. In a crucial moment that is truly pivotal in Mark's gospel, the disciples are traveling with Jesus to the villages around Caesarea Philippi. Along the way, he asks them: "Who do people say I am?" They reply: "Some say John the Baptist; others say Elijah, and still others, one of the prophets." But then Jesus makes it more personal by inquiring, "What about you? Who do you say I am?" Peter answers, "You are the Messiah" (8:27-29).

Most of us are familiar with this story. Peter recognizes Jesus as more than a prophet. Peter is convinced Jesus is the Christ, the Anointed One, the Messiah. We are also likely to know that in Matthew's telling of this particular story Jesus praises Peter for his answer and states that on Peter's confession of faith the very church will be built. But the pattern in the Gospels is unmistakable: a recognition of Jesus as the long-awaited one sent from God is followed by Jesus explaining the necessity of his own suffering and sacrifice.

Mark tells us that following Peter's dramatic confession of faith, "He then began to teach them that the Son of Man must suffer many things and be rejected by the elders, the chief priests and the teachers of the law, and that he must be killed and after three days rise again" (9:31). Peter reacts to this plain speech about impending suffering with protest. Mark uses a strong word to describe Peter's response—a rebuke of Jesus for insisting that he must suffer. In turn Jesus now asks Peter, the one with the heartfelt and insightful confession that Jesus is the Messiah, to "Get behind me, Satan!" (v. 33).

Jesus then calls the disciples close and teaches them:

Whoever wants to be my disciple must deny themselves and take up their cross and follow me. For whoever wants to save their life will lose it, but whoever loses their life for me and for the gospel will save it. What good is it for someone to gain the whole world, yet forfeit their soul? Or what can anyone give in exchange for their soul? (vv. 34-37)

Clearly Jesus saw discipleship as costly. The life and writings of Dietrich Bonhoeffer did not discover the costly nature of discipleship; instead Bonhoeffer's words and deeds are a testimony to his right recognition that it was Jesus who taught us the high cost of discipleship.

Walking with Jesus over a period of some three years, the disciples are reminded of the cost of discipleship time and time again. Reasonable excuses to delay following are not permitted: "You have bought some land?" "You have taken on a new wife?" "You need to first bury your father?" "You have some new livestock?" "You first need to go and say goodbye to your family?" None of these requests for delaying the immediate response of following Jesus are well received.

The disciples see a young man with a track record of keeping the commandments and with a heart that desires to receive God's gift of eternal life be told to take all of his considerable wealth and sell it for the benefit of the poor and then begin the journey of discipleship. When he goes away sorrowful, unwilling at that moment to meet the demands of Jesus, the disciples surely wonder if anyone can be saved with the bar set so high. They bluntly ask Jesus, "Who then can be saved?" (Matt. 19:25).

Jesus answers that "With man this is impossible, but with God all things are possible" (Matt. 19:26). Peter is hopeful that the disciples' level of sacrifice and their willingness to leave work and family and home behind to come and follow Jesus have met the demands of discipleship. Jesus replies, "Everyone who has left houses or brothers or sisters or father or mother or wife or children or fields for my sake will receive a hundred times as much and will inherit eternal life" (v. 28). The demands of discipleship are high, but those willing to pay the price will receive far more than they ever give.

Within the Twelve there is significant jockeying for position. The desire to be "first among equals" seems to be prevalent among the disciples. One day the mother of Zebedee's sons, James and John, comes with them to Jesus seeking favor for her boys. Matthew records the exchange in chapter 20: She wants Jesus to grant her sons a special seat in the kingdom, one to his left and the other to his right. Jesus tells them they do not know the significance of what they are asking. The cup of sacrifice Jesus will soon drink is the path he must take. Are these men ready and willing to join him? Even so, Jesus tells them that decisions about rank in the Kingdom are not his to make; the Father will make those decisions. The other disciples are indignant at James and John for seeking to be exalted above the others. Jesus says to the whole group,

You know the rulers of the Gentiles lord it over them, and their high officials exercise authority over them. Not so with you. Instead, whoever wants to become great among you must be your servant, and whoever wants to be first among you must be your slave—just as the Son of Man did not come to be served, but to serve, and to give his life as a ransom for many. (vv. 25-28)

Jesus repeats this theme throughout his earthly ministry: The first shall be last. The last shall be first. Greatness is defined by service and sacrifice. The sacrificial life of Jesus is a model to be followed. His example of humble service is to be emulated.

We live in a world that rewards success. Media attention and public adulation flow to the rich, the powerful, the famous, and the successful. Jesus absolutely redefines greatness in the kingdom of God. It is a measure of one's willingness to serve others. It is a measure of the degree to which one is willing to sacrifice for the sake of others and for the sake of God's kingdom.

Conveniently, the church has too often offered the benefits and blessings of the Christian life without being up front and clear about the demands of discipleship. Perhaps we have feared that our crowds and membership rolls might thin considerably if we present what Jesus taught about the costs of discipleship. But any serious attempt to discuss the worldview of Jesus must be clear about costly discipleship. And, any efforts to hide these demanding costs from would-be followers of Christ or to give them little attention in our preaching and teaching ministries do a disservice to our hearers. Presenting the invitation to discipleship with all of its risks, costs, and rewards is to take Jesus seriously.

A Call to Ministry

The Gospels record two occasions of Jesus sending out his disciples and followers for ministry. On both occasions Jesus commissions them with instructions for how to carry out their ministry. Luke describes the sending out of the twelve disciples in chapter 9:

> When Jesus had called the Twelve together, he gave them power and authority to drive out all demons and to cure all diseases, and he sent them out to proclaim the kingdom of God and to heal the sick. Take nothing for the journey—no staff, no bag, no bread, no money, no extra shirt. Whatever house you enter, stay there until you leave that town. If people do not welcome you, leave their town and shake the dust off your feet as a testimony against them. (vv. 1-5)

The first thing that catches my attention about these instructions for ministry is that the disciples are to be vulnerable. Ministry is not carried out by making sure we have everything we need. The plans for ministry are quite different from the way the corporate world makes plans for doing business. The wisdom of the world calls for cost/benefit analysis. It is considered folly to venture out without being sure you have the resources you need for success. But with the disciples, Jesus requires a venture of faith.

The disciples do not pack for the journey to be sure they have everything they need. They will travel light—some might say, foolishly light. They must depend on the supportive hospitality of others. They can expect both rejection and opposition. They are not to be alarmed. "Shake the dust off your feet" and move on, Jesus tells them. Jesus faced rejection and opposition. The disciple is not better than the teacher.

The disciples' strength from ministry comes from God. Jesus has granted them the authority to drive out demons and to heal diseases. They are to rely on these provisions from God and not on their own genius, wit, preparation, skill, or talent. Their message is simple and direct: they are to proclaim to all that the kingdom of God is near. There is a new and different way to live, in God's kingdom, a way of life far greater than life in the kingdoms of earth. This is the good news to proclaim.

The second sending of disciples occurs in Luke 10 and involves seventy-two other followers. (This reminds us that Jesus had other followers and disciples in addition to the original twelve.) In pairs they are to go to towns in advance of Jesus visiting those places. Jesus gives these teams of two even fuller instructions for ministry: Like the Twelve, they are to travel light. Jesus refers to their vulnerability when he describes them as "lambs among wolves" (v. 3). They are to be dependent on hospitality. They are to expect hardship and rejection. But their mission of healing the hurts of others and proclaiming to all the inbreaking of God's kingdom is important.

These seventy-two followers return from their first-century mission trips with joy. They are astounded that even the demons submitted to them in Jesus' name. Jesus rejoices with them. In fact, in a rare statement regarding the emotions of Jesus, Luke writes that Jesus is "full of joy through the Holy Spirit" (10:21). We need to see the joy in Christ when his followers are willing to go to the world for ministry and proclamation. When we are willing to be vulnerable and take risks of faith because of our passion to heal hurting persons and to proclaim to all the good news of the nearness of the kingdom of God, we please Jesus.

Jesus ends his time on earth with a commissioning of his disciples to be on mission: "Therefore, go and make disciples of all nations, baptizing them in the name of the Father and of the Son and of the Holy Spirit, and teaching them to obey everything I have commanded you. And surely, I am with you always, to the very end of the age" (Matt. 28:19-20).

By the authority of Christ, we are commissioned to minister in the world as we go. We are to embrace vulnerability. We are to risk what others might deem foolish to risk. We can expect opposition and difficulty on the journey, but the goal is disciple-making. It is proclaiming good news and teaching persons to follow Christ well.

This way of seeing with Christ poses challenges for congregations. We try to be prudent with our ministry and building programs and plans. We don't want to risk too much. We have confused good stewardship with a worldly pragmatism. If there is anything we must honestly confess, it is that we do not find in the Gospels a Jesus vision that supports a movement to build big gathering places for people to meet in his name for worship, study, and fellowship. Now, admittedly in the life of Jesus the synagogue and temple were places for the people of God to gather.

I am not arguing against congregations as places for the people of God to gather for worship and ministry. After all, I am in my forty-third year of serving one congregation. We have built buildings. We gather people for religious purposes. We conduct ministries of benevolence and discipleship. I believe in the church and in congregational ministry. But I do acknowledge that building congregations as strong institutions is not the true aim of God in Christ.

The vision of Christ calls us to go into the world. In the world we are to encounter people where they live. We are to announce the presence of God's kingdom. We are to heal the brokenness and hurts of those we encounter through vulnerable ministry that is wholly dependent on the presence and power of the Holy Spirit. Seeing with Jesus requires the church to view itself as a means to an end, not the end itself.

I am thoroughly captivated by an incarnational view of the church—that we exist to equip sisters and brothers in Christ to go into the world just as Jesus sent the Twelve and the seventy-two in his lifetime. Our purpose in gathering is for the ministries of worshiping and learning that equip us for incarnating the person, message, and ministry of Christ as we go. It is in our scattering into our homes, workplaces, neighborhoods, families, circles of friends and acquaintances and even more, in our willingness to go to people and places that we would not go to were it not for the compelling vision of Jesus, that we live obediently to the one who calls us to the ministry of healing and proclamation in his name.

A Call to Freedom

Any look at how Jesus viewed discipleship needs to take seriously that he never required conformity to custom and form from his followers that the religious legalists of his day expected. The second chapter of Mark introduces some of the questions over the disciples' conduct.

The disciples of John the Baptist are fasting. The Pharisees are fasting. But Jesus and his disciples are not. Jesus defends the disciples by saying, "How can the guests of the bridegroom fast while he is with them? They cannot, so long as they have him with them. But the time will come when the bridegroom will be taken away from them, and on that day they will fast" (Mark 2:19-20). Jesus goes on to talk about new wine needing new wineskins and unshrunk cloth making for a poor patch on a garment. Jesus does not view tradition or public perception as binding on his disciples. They are free to enjoy his presence and the freedom he grants them to love and follow him. Meeting the expectations of how others define piety is of little value to Jesus.

Then, the disciples end up walking through a grain field on the Sabbath. They begin to pick the heads of grain from their clothing. Alas, they have violated the rabbinical teachings on how to keep the Sabbath perfectly. Some busybody Pharisees are interested enough to be bothered by the disciples' Sabbath walk through the field and subsequent picking off the grain—a true example of "knit-picking." Jesus again defends the disciples: "Have you never read what David did when he and his companions were hungry and in need? In the days of Abiathar the high priest, he entered the house of God and ate the consecrated bread, which is lawful only for the priests to eat. And he also gave some to his companions" (Mark 2:25-26).

Clearly to Jesus, the essence of discipleship is found not in strict adherence to religious tradition and custom. The heart of the Law is to be respected and fulfilled. But legalism misses the real point of God's giving us laws and commandments. Jesus sees legalism as a way of promoting oneself. Through extreme piety and moral obedience, one is more likely to become judgmental of others and more prideful than caring. The concern is more for one's reputation than to pleasing God. Jesus views discipleship more as a liberating and joyful inner desire to please God than as conformity to external expectations of piety.

Traveling with Jesus, the disciples hear the critiques of the Pharisees and religious leaders of the day aimed at their Lord: He eats with sinners, heals on the Sabbath, is anointed by a woman of questionable character, and is open to Gentiles. They learn as disciples of Jesus to see law and custom through a different lens.

Obedience to God's will is the heart of law-keeping. But when law-keeping and custom prevent us from doing good or from loving a person made in God's image, we are mistaken. And, when religious piety and moral zeal make us feel superior to others, even cause us to view them as unclean, then we have missed the whole point.

A story told in Luke 18:10-14 surely registers with the disciples. Two men go up to the temple to pray. One is a Pharisee and the other a tax collector. The Pharisee stands by himself and prays, "God, I thank you that I am not like other people—robbers, evildoers, adulterers—or even like this tax collector. I fast twice a week and give a tenth of all I get." But the tax collector stands at a distance and will not even look up to heaven, but beats his breast and says, "God, have mercy on me, a sinner." Jesus comments: "I tell you that this man, rather than the other, went home justified before God. For all those who exalt themselves will be humbled, and those who humble themselves will be exalted."

Clearly, the disciples know that legalism and self-righteousness are not in keeping with Jesus' vision for who they are to be. The piety of the Pharisees is not impressive to Jesus. Their self-congratulations and their rejection of others deemed unworthy are, in fact, an abomination to Christ.

Through the centuries Christians have too often missed this important part of a Jesus worldview. In our love for Christ and our zeal for God—at least we tell ourselves this is our reason—we have ended up living more like the Pharisees than as true followers of Jesus. Any expressions of Christian faith in which we exalt ourselves as believers and condemn and exclude others for their sinful lives because they do not measure up to our standards are, in fact, distortions of true faith as Jesus envisioned.

A Call to Faith

The power and energy for the disciples to live into Jesus' vision for them will come through faith. Throughout the Gospels the disciples marvel at how Jesus can do so much and question how they can even think of doing what Christ seems confident they can do. Just as persistently, Jesus models for them an unwavering faith in God and persistently calls them to simply believe, to have faith. Jesus praises the faith he sees in others and lifts their example to the disciples:

- A Roman centurion desires to see his servant healed. He does not expect Jesus to come to his home, but trusts that Jesus can simply say the word and his servant will live.
- Jesus sees the faith of friends who bring a paralyzed man to him for healing.
- A discouraged woman, sick for many years, reaches out to touch the hem of Jesus' garment.
- Two blind men believe Jesus can restore their sight.
- A Canaanite woman shows extraordinary humility in begging for Jesus to heal her daughter.
- A father believes Jesus can restore a son that the disciples could not restore.

In all of these encounters Jesus wants his disciples to recognize the faith in the individuals who trusted him, who believed he could do anything for them. He wants his disciples to have just such a faith, and he repeatedly points out to the disciples their lack of faith and trust and how this hinders their capacity to do all that God can do through them:

- When the disciples are concerned that they might perish in a storm on the sea, they find Jesus asleep in the stern of the boat. They impatiently ask, "Teacher, don't you care if we drown?" Jesus gets up and rebukes the wind and says to the waves, "Quiet! Be still!" After the wind dies down and the sea is calm, Jesus asks his disciples: "Why are you so afraid? Do you still have no faith?" (Mark 4:38-40).

• On another difficult night on the water the disciples see Jesus walking on the sea. Peter is even able to take a few unimaginable steps toward Jesus before he falters and lands in the sea. He cries out to Jesus for help. The Lord reaches out his hand to catch Peter and then responds: "You of little faith, why did you doubt?" (Matt. 14:31).

• In the stories of the feeding of the multitudes, the disciples want Jesus to send the crowds away. They are hungry and the disciples see no possible way for so many to be fed. Yet, Jesus insists that the disciples give the crowds something to eat. They must bring what they have, even if only a few loaves of bread and some fish, and trust that Jesus can feed the people. They must have faith! (How surprised they must have been to collect twelve baskets of leftovers to help feed others after everyone had eaten and been satisfied.)

• In John 11, Jesus encourages a grieving Martha to have faith, to believe in him, her brother might be restored to life.

• In talking with his disciples in the upper room, Jesus encourages them to face the possibility of his leaving them with faith and trust: "You believe in God, believe also in me" (John 14:1). Jesus is to be trusted; he alone is the way to the Father, and there are ample rooms in the Father's house for all. The disciples simply must have faith.

• Jesus teaches his disciples that "everything is possible for one who believes" (Mark 9:23). After Jesus curses a fig tree that bears no fruit, the next day the disciples discover the tree is withered up from the roots. They marvel that Jesus' words have truly cursed the barren, but previously green tree. He answers them simply, "Have faith in God" (Mark 11:22).

• With faith the disciples can say to the mountain to be cast into the sea, and it will happen. Jesus encourages them not to "doubt in their heart." For Jesus, the locus of faith is in the heart. This faith applies to the disciples' prayer lives. If they will pray from hearts full of faith, they will see prayers answered.

• When the apostles ask Jesus to "Increase our faith," he replies: "If you have faith as small as a mustard seed, you can say to this mulberry tree, be uprooted and planted in the sea and it will obey you" (Luke 17:5-6). Have the faith of a mustard seed; understand that a little leaven can leaven the whole loaf. Jesus is calling his disciples to be persons of unwavering faith and remarkable trust.

In the post-Enlightenment world, culture valued proof. Reason worshiped at the altar of facts. That world has undergone great shifts as we enter a new age. But many Christian voices resist the move into a world not so certain of facts and not so enamored of proof. Much of fundamentalism is a stubborn resistance to see faith move from the modern to a post-modern world. Thus, we hear Christian faith discussed as being provable.

Faith in the Creator is replaced with arguments that creationism is scientific and proven by evidence. Faith that God speaks through Scripture is replaced by argument for inerrant writings literally dictated by God in the original manuscripts. Faith in Jesus is replaced by rational assent to propositional truths. Intellectual believing in the propositions of some four spiritual laws and a transactional, public adherence to these truths become the path to salvation, not the path of grace through faith.

Listen to the rhetoric: you will hear a repeated emphasis on knowing, not on trusting with faith. This new cult of "knowing" is as old as the ancient Gnostic heresies. There has always been a temptation to view Christian belief as knowledge for insiders that emphasizes knowing over believing, knowing over trusting, and knowing over following.

For Christian faith to thrive meaningfully in our world, we must see true discipleship more like Jesus and less like the propositional and transactional faith many of us learned in evangelical churches or from high-profile preachers and teachers with national audiences. Here is what Jesus taught about discipleship:

It is an invitation from God, a call to follow. It is costly and sacrificial, but it is worth the price of faithful following. The disciple is to minister and serve, to heal and comfort, following the example of Jesus. Discipleship is not being bound to religious law and custom, but it is being set free to serve others in Jesus' name. Ultimately, the power of discipleship is measured by the degree of faith inside the disciple. We are called to simply believe, to trust, to have faith in our innermost being. That faith is what carries us into the world to do the work of and to bear witness to the kingdom of God.

For those worried about the future of the church and even the Christian faith itself, the remedy is to see discipleship clearly. Faithful followers of Christ are still being called to go into the world; to announce the good news of the arriving kingdom of God; to heal the hurting and bind up the brokenhearted; to live a risky, even difficult life, empowered by an inner faith that trusts God with all one's heart. My prayer is that some of the turbulence we see in the church today is hopefully a rejection of our inauthentic forms of worship and practice in the modern world and a transition to a rediscovery of seeing discipleship with Jesus.

A Call to Prayer

We read in the Scriptures how Jesus models for his disciples the way to protect, preserve, and strengthen their faith through prayer. When the crowds press in and Jesus grows weary, he values getting away, being alone, and devoting himself to prayer. Sometimes pressing needs interrupt his efforts, but Jesus makes it clear to his disciples that the energy needed for following God's will in the world comes from prayer. They request of him, "Lord, teach us to pray." They want to experience what Jesus experiences in prayer.

The inner circle of Peter, James, and John are privileged to know the importance of retreat and prayer to Jesus. They discover this at the Mount of Transfiguration and in the Garden of Gethsemane. All of the disciples hear the beautiful intimacy of Jesus with God the Father in his prayer for them uttered from the upper room and recorded in John 17. They see the zeal with which he cleanses the temple and his insistence that the temple, his Father's house, should be a house of prayer.

It is also noteworthy that worship in community matters to Jesus. The gospel texts tell us that going to the synagogue on the Sabbath is his custom. His pilgrimages to Jerusalem reflect his keeping of the traditional feasts of the Jewish faith. I am always moved in worship on Maundy Thursday when I read his words, "I have eagerly desired to eat this Passover with you before I suffer" (Luke 22:15). On the eve of his great ordeal of sacrifice, keeping Passover with his disciples means something to Jesus.

This final section on discipleship is meant to be a helpful warning against trying to follow Jesus through constant activism. In our world today some people are ready to jettison communal worship, prayer, and other spiritual disciplines, and the celebration of high and holy days as unnecessary. They want to be crusaders for justice and actively engaged in mission and ministry, with little regard for personal or communal spiritual formation. This is not the example Jesus set for discipleship. In the call to follow there is definitely a call to go and serve. But there is also a call to prayer. True discipleship understands the wisdom of Christ and balances prayer and worship with ministry and service.

Questions for Discussion/Reflection

1. Think of how you and your church extend an invitation to others to become a part of the Christian community. Is it more of an invitation to give assent to certain truths about salvation? Is it more of a simple invitation to participate in spiritual community? Or, is it more of an invitation to become a follower of Jesus? If the latter, does your church life keep at the forefront the goal of effective discipleship through mutual encouragement of one another?

2. In what ways have you found discipleship to be truly costly? Are you surprised, perhaps, that your faith has not really been too costly to you? If so, why do you think that may be? Do you sometimes wonder if the ease of our discipleship may be an indication that we may not have taken real discipleship seriously enough; that we may not have really progressed too far at all in following Jesus?

3. Are you concerned enough about our excuses for delayed discipleship? Jesus was pretty harsh on those with excuses for delaying their following him. Some of their excuses seem far more reasonable than our own. What might Jesus need to say to you?

4. How do you react to the idea of true discipleship as "the impossible possibility"? Is this a reasonable explanation of your own discipleship?

5. Comment on the idea of discipleship as going into the world as opposed to coming to church. Does your church keep this distinction clear? How do

you react to the idea of an incarnational view of the church, that we come together to equip and encourage one another to go out into the world to make disciples even as we live as disciples? How might viewing your congregation as an incarnational church affect your approach to ministry?

6. How do you describe the difference between how true disciples of Jesus and religious legalists such as the Pharisees view issues of keeping scriptural commandments and established religious practices? How would you rate your efforts at living like a true disciple as opposed to someone such as a Pharisee? How can the church change its perception in the culture that we are pharisaical, judgmental, and legalistic?

7. Comment on your own faith journey. How hard has it been to keep faith? Has faith been the energy and passion that fuels your discipleship? How can you and your church strive to find that "faith of a mustard seed"?

8. How well do you balance the need for prayer, retreat, and worship with the call of Christ to go and serve? How well does your Christian community balance spiritual formation with incarnational ministry in the world?

CHAPTER 3

Seeing in His Encounters

If you really want to get know the character of a person, watch how they treat others. It is easy to talk a good game of compassion and generosity, of kindness and service. But sometimes our actions belie the real truth of who we really are.

How do you treat the person who cuts in front of you in line? How do you treat your spouse and children in the privacy of your home? How do you react to persons who by their look and demeanor are quite different from you? How do you deal with the beggar who asks for your help? How do you respond to challenge and criticism? How do you tip the waitress or waiter who serves your breakfast? How willing are you to visit an elderly person who is lonely? How does your behavior change in times of stress?

The Gospels give us ample insight into seeing Jesus through his encounters with others. If we as Christians are going to talk about the right treatment of the poor, of women, of the oppressed, of the neglected, we should surely let our guide be the way Jesus treated these persons. In a divided and often angry world where we find ourselves in arguments at the family table at holidays, with friends on social media, and with persons who sit beside us in Sunday school classes or in worship, we need to see how Jesus treated those who opposed him and those with whom he had substantial differences of opinion.

Seeing Jesus with His Family

The Gospels tell us almost nothing about Jesus as a boy, an adolescent, or a young adult. The one story we have concerns the visit of his family to the temple for the Festival of the Passover when Jesus is twelve. His recorded age is significant, for this is the time he is coming into recognition as one of the men of Israel.

Travel to Jerusalem is communal, in caravan style, so it is not surprising that Jesus might not be alongside his parents as the travelers are returning home. But after a day of travel, Mary and Joseph are concerned. They return to Jerusalem to find Jesus engaged in dialogue with the elders. His questions and answers have everyone amazed. Mary is exasperated at his treatment of his parents, having caused them great concern when they found he was not traveling home with them. Young Jesus responds, "Why were you searching for me? Didn't you know I had to be in my Father's house?" (Luke 2:49). Then Jesus returns with his parents and is obedient to them. A beautiful summary statement follows that can be a model for any youth seeking to follow Jesus well: "And Jesus grew in wisdom and stature, in favor with God and man" (v. 52).

Jesus is a normal boy, respectful and obedient. Yet, already he is keenly aware of a greater reverence and obedience with a claim on his life, directed to God, the Father. In baptism his sonship with God is beautifully affirmed as a voice from heaven sounds as he comes up from the water, "This is my Son, whom I love; with him I am well pleased" (Matt. 3:17).

At the onset of his ministry we learn of a day Jesus spends with his mother, Mary, attending a wedding in Cana. Mary prompts Jesus to act when she tells him they have run out of wine. It is hard to know the tone with which these words are shared, but Jesus says, "Woman, why do you involve me? My hour has not yet come" (John 2:4). Whether said in a teasing or perturbed manner, Jesus responds to her request: the ceremonial washing pots are filled to the brim, and the waiters draw exquisite wine from them.

At home in the Nazareth synagogue Jesus announces the intention of his ministry. Quoting Isaiah, he says, "The Spirit of the Lord is upon me, because he has anointed me to proclaim good news to the poor. He has sent me to proclaim freedom for the prisoners, and recovery of sight to the blind, to set the oppressed free, to proclaim the year of the Lord's favor" (Luke 4:18-19). Jesus declares to his family and neighbors: "Today this scripture is fulfilled in your hearing" (v. 21).

The hometown crowd is astir. How can Joseph's son make such a claim? Most of the locals are impressed by his gracious words, impressed by his wisdom. But when Jesus lets them know that Nazareth will receive no special blessings from him, agreeing with the old wisdom that a prophet is not accepted in his hometown, they turn on him. In fury the people of Nazareth are ready to run him off the side of the cliff. This could not have been easy for Mary and his brothers and sisters. Mark records that in the early stages of his ministry, when his family hears about this, they go to take charge of Jesus, saying, "He is out of his mind" (3:20).

Later in his Galilean ministry his mother and brothers come to see Jesus. The crowds surrounding him make it impossible for them to enter the place where he is speaking. Jesus is told that his mother and brothers are waiting outside to see him. Jesus counters, "My mother and brothers are those who hear God's word and put it into practice" (Luke 8:21). His words seem harsh, and they probably sting Mary and his brothers. But they point again to how Jesus sees family. His views mean no harm, neglect, nor disrespect to his earthly family. But Jesus is intent on celebrating the family of God here on earth—a family of persons devoted to God and obedient to God, brothers and sisters united not by blood but by shared faith.

Mary is faithfully present for the darkest moment of her son's life. Along with her sister and Mary Magdalene, she witnesses his cruel death on the cross. Jesus takes note of her presence, as recorded in John's gospel: "When Jesus saw his mother standing there, and the disciple whom he loved standing nearby, he said to her, 'Woman, here is your son,' and to the disciple, 'Here is your mother.' From that time on, this disciple took her into his home" (19:26-27). The bondservant of the Lord, who has obediently carried Jesus and given birth to him, is now with him in death. The affection between mother and son is clearly evident.

What do we learn from seeing Jesus relate to his family? First, the very fact that Matthew and Luke introduce their birth narratives into their gospels tells us that Mary and Joseph are not insignificant. A visit from God to earth did not require that the visit begin as all other lives begin—born as an infant. But a part of the great mystery of the incarnation is that Jesus has an earthly family. His obedience as a child and respect for his parents are documented. But his highest allegiance is to God, not to family. Jesus knows that he must be about "his Father's business."

Second, in his teachings, Jesus is clear about the sanctity of marriage. He clearly rebukes the Jewish practice of some men to get around their vows of marriage by utilizing the Law's allowances to give a wife a certificate of divorce. But Jesus never elevates family to a place or position that meeting their expectations limits his complete obedience to the will of the Father who sent him to earth. He does not accept family excuses for delayed obedience or partial discipleship.

When I went to Zebulon, North Carolina, as a young 22-year-old youth minister, there was a precocious young man in the youth group, a ninth grader at the time. We became close through my years as his youth minister and have remained close through the ensuing years. He is now a trusted friend and colleague, an exceptional pastor now for more than thirty years. As a seminarian, from 1985–1988, he was single. He was full of opinions he freely expressed. One had to do with the Southern Baptist Convention's emphasis on marriage, family, and sexual purity. I will never forget his stinging critique: "They have made the Christian family the fourth person of the Trinity."

When I listen to voices professing their biblical worldview today, I often wonder if they have not made the same error. So much of their emphasis of a biblical worldview continues to be focused on the sanctity of marriage, a hierarchical vision of the family, and an emphasis on sexual purity. Their greatest concerns seem to be on the breakdown of family values in the culture.

I do not find anything in the teachings and practices of Jesus that disregards the value of family. Mary and Joseph did a good work in loving Jesus and providing him an earthly family. His affection for his mother seems unquestioned. But for Jesus the kingdom of God is much broader than a cultural movement to strengthen traditional families. There are brothers and sisters to be embraced outside the home and family. The greatest kinship is the kinship of the human family, especially with those motivated by love for and obedience to God.

"Anyone who loves their father or mother more than me is not worthy of me; anyone who loves their son or daughter more than me is not worthy of me" (John 10:37). Just prior to this verse Jesus states an unavoidable truth: for some, his coming will divide families. Those of us raised in Christian homes, steeped in Christian tradition, find this hard to understand and accept. But indeed, many families have been closed to the idea of a member embracing the call to follow Jesus, to become a disciple. And, many times courageous disciples have not allowed that resistance to keep them from following the Lord.

In striving to adopt a Jesus worldview consistent with the gospel, we need not diminish the importance of family relationships. But a worldview consistent with the Jesus revealed in the Gospels will be careful about elevating home and family to a priority far greater than Jesus did. Any view of the kingdom of God built around our definitions of traditional family that excludes those outside of families who look like our model is deficient. Also deficient is any concept of discipleship that puts one's earthly family above the family of God and makes excuses for family reasons for less than complete obedience to do the will and work of God.

Seeing Jesus with Satan

Following his baptism, we are told in Matthew 4 that the Spirit drives Jesus out into the wilderness. He experiences a period of fasting and prayer for forty days. Jesus is following a tradition of many mystical, spiritual figures of his day and age. The wilderness is a place for testing. Through aloneness, prayer and fasting, one would ultimately encounter and be challenged by the demons that would seek to defeat one's spirit. Only after this period of wrestling with oneself, with temptation, and even with the forces of evil could one emerge tested and ready to provide spiritual insight to others.

As the period of forty days ends, an exhausted Jesus is tempted by Satan. Experiencing the pangs of deep hunger, the first temptation is to turn stones into bread, to feed the deep physical urge he surely feels after such a prolonged fast. Jesus responds to Satan's challenge with "It is written, 'Man shall not live by bread alone, but on every word that comes from the mouth of God'" (Matt. 4:4).

The second temptation involves proving for all to see his special protection promised from God by throwing himself from the pinnacle of the temple, confident that angels will keep him from harm. Noting that Jesus is using Scripture in his response, the tempter bases his argument on Scripture, too. Jesus says, "It is also written, 'Do not put the Lord your God to the test'" (Matt. 4:7).

With the final temptation, Jesus is shown and promised all of the kingdoms of this world to be given with only one condition: that Jesus bow down and worship this devil. Jesus rebukes him, saying, "Away from me, Satan! For it is written, 'Worship the Lord your God, and serve him only'" (Matt. 4:10).

I remember many years ago coming across the text of a sermon preached by Vance Havner on "The Threefold Temptation of the Church." I remember the sermon well, though I have long misplaced it or it is filed where I cannot retrieve it. Based on this text recounting the temptation of Christ, Havner expressed his belief that the church faces the same three temptations: to get into the bread business, show business, and political business.

Vance Havner was not criticizing food pantries or feeding ministries by the church when he warned against the temptation to get into the bread business. He was describing a far more subtle temptation to "feed" persons what they want to hear. It is easy to make ministry choices that give people what they want. It is easy to preach and teach Scripture in such a way that reinforces traditions and customs that defend the status quo. It can be an enticing path to ministry success to tickle the ears of parishioners with what they want to hear as opposed to calling them to biblical truth. Churches that give in to the temptation to turn stones to bread are ones craving measurable ministry success over faithfulness, that prefer keeping members comfortable rather than challenging them with the demands of discipleship.

The tempting appeal of show business is obvious. The idea of the church as a center for religious entertainment pervades the American church scene. While we have waged "worship wars" over issues of style, the world has increasingly ignored our message as lacking substance. The lavish expenditures of the church on building and equipping our "theaters" for entertaining the masses in worship is embarrassing compared to what we invest in doing the work of the kingdom of God as we mend the broken and heal the hurting.

Surely we can recognize how much of the church in the late twentieth and early twenty-first century has given in to the temptation of entering the political business. Pastors with national reputations jockey for position to be spiritual advisors, welcome in the Rose Garden or in other places of power and authority. Is it not interesting that Satan could offer to Jesus the kingdoms of this world? We have devolved into divided Christian camps that express our Christian and biblical worldview in ways that sound incredibly like the campaign messages of either conservative Republicans or liberal Democrats. Neither of these political worldviews are identical with the worldview of Jesus expressed in the Gospels. But some of the political rhetoric expressed as defending a biblical worldview is downright contradictory to the teachings of Christ.

Jesus fought his own temptations by being true to Scripture. We live not by bread only, but by the word of God. We do not need to tempt our God. We must worship and serve our God alone. The distortions we hear today so incorrectly labeled as a biblical or Christian worldview can only be corrected by following the example of Jesus in confronting temptation. Stay true to the word of God, for a Jesus worldview depends on what we know of Jesus from the Gospels. Stay true to the message of Christ and live by it, whether it is popular or not. And, be undivided in your allegiance to the Lord.

Divided allegiances to earthly kingdoms lead us to compromise the teachings of Jesus and contort them to fit our political and social systems. Faith is distorted and discipleship is weakened when we make our political views and social views dominant and use Christ to defend our positions. To live with a Jesus worldview, our faith will inform our political and social preferences and understandings. But these views cannot become so central to us that our allegiance to God and to following Jesus is in any way compromised.

Seeing Jesus with Children

It is worthwhile to see the way Jesus related to children. Jesus understood children and their games. I love the story of the children playing in the marketplace, recorded in Matthew 11.

Jesus has been talking about John the Baptist. The critics of John's ascetic lifestyle condemn him as demon-possessed. The critics of Jesus and of his willingness to celebrate life with sinners and receive their hospitality lead them to view him as a drunkard and glutton.

To explain his frustration with the critics, Jesus tells them, "To what shall I compare this generation? They are like children sitting in the marketplaces and calling out to others, 'We played the pipe for you and you did not dance; we sang a dirge, and you did not mourn'" (Matt. 11:16-17). Jesus is aware that children are left alone in the marketplace to entertain themselves while their mothers buy and sell.

Two possibilities for imaginative play are weddings and funerals. The children play-act the times when the community ccomes together, either to celebrate the marriage of a young couple or to mourn the passing of a dear loved one. Alas, the children just refuse to play. We play the pipe to reenact a wedding celebration, but no one dances. We sing a dirge as a call to act out a somber funeral processional, but no one plays the role of mourner.

Jesus uses this story of children to critique his generation. In his view, we should be willing to embrace both celebration and mourning. We are to dance at weddings. We are to mourn at funerals. Here the church has a great opportunity to minister to our communities. Embracing the joyous celebration of life and mourning the truly lamentable things worth mourning are indeed the task of the church. Any unwillingness of pious people to celebrate or mourn is inexcusable. Children in the marketplace can teach us that much.

As the crowds bring little children to Jesus for him to bless them and lay hands on them, well-meaning disciples try to protect their busy master by shooing away the children and their parents. Their actions intended to protect Jesus earn them a sharp rebuke: "Let the little children come to me, and do not hinder them, for the kingdom of God belongs to such as these. Truly I tell you, anyone who will not receive the kingdom of God like a little child will never enter it" (Mark 10:14-15).

How beautiful to envision Jesus motioning the children to come to him, to see him delight in blessing them. We need to hear and heed his words. Children are not a nuisance to be herded away. God's kingdom belongs to children. In fact, we must become as children to enter God's kingdom. That takes humility, faith, and trust—all exemplified by the wide-eyed wonder of a child.

In Matthew 18 the disciples want to know who will be considered greatest in the kingdom of heaven. In response, Jesus calls a little child to come to him and says:

> Truly I tell you, unless you change and become like little children, you will never enter the kingdom of heaven. Therefore, whoever takes the lowly position of this child is the greatest in the kingdom of heaven. And whoever welcomes one such child in my name welcomes me. If anyone causes one of these little ones—those who believe in me—to stumble, it would be better for them to have a large millstone hung around their neck and to be drowned in the depths of the sea. Woe to the world because of the things that cause people to stumble! (vv. 3-7)

Again, the child is lifted up as the model for the kingdom subject. But in this text, more is added. Welcoming and receiving a child is in itself a welcoming of Jesus. But rejecting a child, causing that child to stumble, is a woeful, lamentable mistake. A Jesus worldview will have a heart for children—a welcoming, loving, and appreciative heart. Children will be cared for and noticed. Their needs will be met. They will be loved.

In January of 2020, our pastor responsible for leading our congregation's mission efforts told me of a call from the social services office warning us to expect a rise in persons seeking help from our food ministry, as 750,000 persons were being removed from the food stamp program and another 1,500,000 would be dropped in the coming months. I could not help but think of this as I write about Jesus and children. It really would be better to be thrown into the sea with a heavy weight around your neck than to decide it is best to feed fewer hungry children, especially if you try to defend decisions like these as consistent with a biblical or Christian worldview. These actions are simply not compatible with a Jesus worldview.

"Your Father in heaven is not willing that any of these little ones should perish" (Matt. 18:14). Christians who are serious about a Jesus worldview must be serious about loving children. Of course, God will take care of the little children. God will extend the joy of the kingdom to the little ones. We do not worry about the eternal destiny of children, for they are securely held by the hands of a loving God. But the perishing of a child on this earth displeases God greatly.

Children lack clean water, good food, shelter, protection, and adequate medical care—God weeps that children are perishing. Quality education suffers for poor children in the re-segregation of schools, orchestrated by Christians in the name of parental choice and deemed consistent with a biblical worldview. But it is not alright with God. Children matter to God. And, all children and their welfare will matter greatly to anyone serious about being a follower of Jesus.

As a child I was taught to sing "Jesus loves me, this I know, for the Bible tells me so." But I was also taught, "Jesus loves the little children, all the children of the world." The dear ladies who taught me to sing these songs at Moreland Avenue Baptist Church in Atlanta, Georgia were doing well, helping me as a child to see children the way Jesus saw children—all the children of the world.

Seeing Jesus with Women

The role of women in the church, home, and society has been much debated by Christians through the years. How women are to be treated and respected can become a dividing line among Christians, as believers in Christ choose different ways of viewing the role of women.

You will not find in the teachings of Jesus long discourse on his views with regard to women and their rights. He lived in a male-dominated, patriarchal society. There were no groups fighting for the rights of women to align with in his day and age. But in a world where women were too easily dismissed and ignored, Jesus seemed open and eager to minister to women; to see them and understand their need; to offer them healing, grace, and encouragement. That, in and of itself, speaks volumes about how Jesus viewed women.

I love the stories of dialogue between Jesus and women found in John's gospel. The first I will mention is the encounter with the woman at the well of Jacob near Sychar in Samaria. There is every reason for Jesus to avoid her. She is a woman. It is not the norm for men to approach women in conversation. She is a Samaritan; Jesus is a Jew. Their people do not get along; they do not mix. Their religious beliefs have some points of contact but also differ widely, and the two groups have little appreciation or respect for the other's religious practices. And then, there is the issue of this woman's morals: five husbands and now living with a man outside of marriage—what a scandal!

Yet, Jesus talks with her. A conversation asking her to give him a drink surprises her. They banter back and forth, probing and testing one another. Ultimately it all leads to conversation about God, and Jesus reveals to the woman that he is the Messiah she says will come. Jesus is willing to set aside all the things that divide them to offer the hope of true worship: "Yet a time is coming and has now come when the true worshipers will worship the Father in the Spirit and in truth, for they are the kind of worshipers the Father seeks. God is spirit, and his worshipers must worship in the Spirit and in truth" (John 4:23-24).

The disciples are taken aback by the willingness of Jesus to engage this woman. But while they stumble around with their own struggling perceptions of Jesus in their early days of following him, this woman has become quite the evangelist. The text is clear: "Many of the Samaritans from that town believed in him because of the woman's testimony" (John 4:39). Yet, many people today still question any willingness to hear the preaching of the gospel by a woman. One must wonder how a story like this fits that particular worldview.

In chapter 8 John tells of another encounter. A woman is caught in the act of adultery, and her accusers are following the Law to execute her by stoning. The Pharisees find this a delightful trap for Jesus, seeking his opinion on her pending execution. If he opposes the stoning, Jesus will reveal his contempt for following the Law. If he blesses her execution, Jesus will not seem so gentle and compassionate to the multitude. Jesus survives their trap. "Let anyone of you who is without sin be the first to throw a stone at her" (v. 7).

The crowd goes silent. The older Pharisees are the first to drop their rocks and walk away. Eventually everyone leaves Jesus alone with the woman. Jesus has shown his compassion for a woman who has sinned, rescuing her from the angry execution of a self-righteous mob. His word to her is a word of grace: "Then neither do I condemn you. Go now and leave your life of sin" (John 8:11).

Mary and Martha, along with their brother Lazarus, are friends of Jesus. Their home in Bethany has been a place where Jesus has enjoyed their hospitality. On one occasion Martha expresses her frustration with Mary. While Martha is busy preparing and serving food, Mary is sitting at the feet of Jesus, hanging on to his every word. Jesus responds, "Martha, Martha, you are worried and upset about many things, but few things are needed—or indeed only one. Mary has chosen what is better, and it will not be taken away from her" (Luke 10:41-42).

There is no lack of appreciation for Martha's hospitality in his response. But Jesus is making an important point with truly significant impact. Mary is welcome to sit beside him and hear his teaching. The woman has a place in the company of men to hear talk and teaching about God and God's kingdom. Her place is not relegated to the kitchen; her role is not limited to the care and feeding of the men.

Surely Martha appreciates this teaching when Jesus takes time to talk with her at the occasion of her brother's death. In the midst of her grief Jesus talks to Martha about truly important things: "I am the resurrection and the life. The one who believes in me will live, even though they die; and whoever lives by believing in me will never die. Do you believe this?" (John 11:25-26). Truly one of the most important theological conversations to ever take place is this one between Jesus and Martha. He challenges her to believe in him, and she does.

In another encounter, Jesus sees the lifeless body of the only son of a widowed woman being carried out of the town gate in a place called Nain. His heart goes out to the woman, and he speaks words of comfort: "Don't cry" (Luke 7:13). The vulnerability of a widow who has lost her only son is great in that culture. Jesus calls the young man back to life. "The dead man sat up, and began to talk, and Jesus gave him back to his mother" (Luke 7:15).

Luke's gospel also records this touching story: With an alabaster jar of perfume in hand a woman with a notorious, sinful reputation comes into the home of a Pharisee who has invited Jesus to dinner. Her tears wet Jesus' feet, then she wipes her tears with her hair before anointing Jesus' feet with the expensive perfume. The Pharisee is indignant at the display and questions the authenticity of Jesus as one sent from God: "If this man were a prophet, he would know who is touching him and what kind of woman that she is—that she is a sinner" (Luke 7:39). Jesus challenges his host and defends the woman, offering to her the grace of forgiveness.

In the next chapter of Luke an opportunity is presented to Jesus. A synagogue leader, Jairus, begs for Jesus to come to his home. His twelve-year-old daughter is dying. This is an opportunity to bring healing to the child of a person of prominence. Making his way through the crowd, Jesus stops. Someone has touched him.

Luke lets us know the person who reaches out to touch Jesus is a woman, suffering with continual bleeding for a dozen years. In her condition, she is considered "unclean" in the eyes of the Jewish law, Yet, Jesus stops his trek toward the house of Jairus. He wants to know who has touched him.

"The woman, seeing that she could not go unnoticed, came trembling and fell at his feet. In the presence of all the people, she told why she had touched him and how she had been instantly healed" (Luke 8:47). Jesus replies to her, "Daughter, your faith has healed you. Go in peace" (v. 48).

By now the word comes: The little girl is dead. There is no need to bother Jesus. The opportunity has been lost to work a miracle for the family of a synagogue leader. Jesus insists on going to the home and that the little girl will be healed. With compassion and kindness, he calls the little one to rise from her deathbed: "My child, get up" (Luke 8:54). The daughter is restored to life and to her family.

Earlier in Luke 8 we learn that women are welcome to travel with Jesus and the twelve disciples. And, we learn of their willingness to share their own resources in support of the ministry of Jesus and the Twelve:

After this, Jesus traveled about from one town and village to another, proclaiming the good news of the kingdom of God. The Twelve were with him, and also some women who had been cured of evil spirits and diseases. Mary (called Magdalene) from whom seven demons had come out; Joanna, the wife of Chuza, the manager of Herod's household; Susanna; and many others. These women were helping to support him out of their own means. (vv. 1-3)

Throughout his travels, Jesus continues to minister to women. Risking the usual indignation of his opponents for healing on the Sabbath, he heals a woman who is severely bent over, crippled in that painful condition for eighteen years. With compassion he tells her, "Woman, you are free from your infirmity" (Luke 13:12). A Gentile woman seeks help from Jesus. Her little girl is possessed by an impure spirit. In a back-and-forth exchange in which the words of Jesus seem to lack their usual compassion, the Syrophoenician woman is unrelenting. Undaunted by his reference to "dogs," she makes it clear that she can be humble enough to accept, like a dog, any crumbs that may fall from his table. Jesus likes her reply and rewards her persistence: "For such a reply you may go; the demon has left your daughter" (Mark 7:29).

The record in the Gospels is consistent. The plight of women moves Jesus to compassion. And, Jesus is willing to bring healing and restoration to women and their loved ones.

With the disciples scattered in fear and confusion, faithful women stand by Jesus at the time of his death. And on the morning of resurrection, women come to the tomb with spices to anoint the body of Jesus. They are the first to encounter the empty tomb and the words announcing that Jesus is alive. They are the first to see the risen Christ, and the ones trusted to bear the good news of resurrection to the disciples.

The Gospels do not cast Jesus as a twenty-first-century feminist. The culture of his day and age was so different from ours. But the evidence in his encounters with women is heavily weighted to depict Jesus as a friend of women and a rare man willing to welcome women into his inner circle and to accept their partnership in ministry.

Jesus clearly felt compassion for women who were mistreated and discarded by religious law and tradition. It was his desire to bring healing and restoration to them. It is actually quite striking to see the number of encounters with women recorded in the Gospels. One would expect a prominent religious leader in Jesus' day to have been dismissive of women and unwilling to engage women considered unclean, immoral, or outside the Jewish nation. But in the brief record of Jesus' encounters in the four gospels, women occupy a far greater role than anyone aware of the customs of his time would predict.

Seeing Jesus with Persons Who Sought Him

We cannot mention all the many encounters with persons who came to Jesus seeking healing for themselves or for others or questioning Jesus about spiritual matters. But perhaps a quick summary of several significant encounters can help us to see how Jesus related to persons in his interactions with them.

Early in Mark's gospel a man with leprosy approaches Jesus. He begs him, "If you are willing, you can make me clean" (1:40). Questioning his willingness to heal causes Jesus to be indignant, according to Mark. Jesus is presented in the Gospels as a man of compassion, clearly willing to bring healing from disease, relief from suffering, and restoration to those who have experienced rejection and scorn. Jesus heals in different ways. Sometimes he simply declares them healed and well. Sometimes he gives them instructions for healing. In this case, defying the custom that forbids touching the unclean leper, Jesus reaches out his hand and touches the man (v. 41).

In the land of the Gerasenes a man with an impure spirit inhabits the tombs. His violent nature requires that he be bound in the tombs. He is a frightening man, crying out from those tombs in anguish, cutting himself with stones. In his encounter with Christ the demons within the man recognize Jesus and beg for mercy. They admit that these unclean spirits are "Legion" within this poor man. Jesus calls them out of the man and, as the story goes, they head for a herd of swine that promptly drown themselves in the lake. This awesome encounter with whatever makes a person so troubled and anguished is frightening. Persons who have grown to expect the bizarre behavior from this man are even more frightened by the new reality, as they see him "sitting, there, dressed and in his right mind" (Mark 5:15). The man begs Jesus to allow him to come and travel with him. Life as the "former demoniac" in his own village seems a less-than-inviting proposition. But Jesus prefers that the man stay in his home and bear witness to what the Lord has done for his life.

Luke records the healing of ten lepers as Jesus travels the border between Samaria and Galilee. The men cry to Jesus for pity on their dreadful plight. He instructs them, "Go show yourselves to the priests" (17:14). As they travel along the way, they discover that they are indeed cleansed. Going to the priests to validate their healing will restore them to family and community. Alas, but there is no Jewish priest to perform any rituals of reconciliation for one of the ten, for he is a Samaritan. Instead he comes back to express his heartfelt thanks, throwing himself at Jesus' feet. Jesus appreciates the return of this one, the foreigner, to give thanks and praise to God. The man receives more than just healing from leprosy as Jesus commands him to "Rise, and go, your faith has made you well" (v. 19).

In Jericho a despised tax collector wants to see Jesus. Climbing a tree to see Jesus pass by, Jesus confronts the man: "Zacchaeus, come down immediately. I must stay at your house today" (Luke 19:5). Jesus invariably notices the one whom others ignore; he invariably includes the one whom others exclude. He opens himself up to receive hospitality from those considered unclean and unworthy. He comes to the house of Zacchaeus and announces, "Today, salvation has come to this house, because this man, too, is a son of Abraham. For the Son of Man came to seek and to save the lost" (vv. 9-10). The conversion in Zacchaeus is extraordinary. At the onset of a new life as a follower of Jesus, he pledges half of all he possesses for the relief of the poor and promises to repay fourfold any and all who he has cheated.

Nicodemus is a Pharisee, a member of the Sanhedrin. In the darkness of night he comes to see Jesus, saying, "Rabbi, we know that you are a teacher who has come from God. For no one could perform the signs you are doing if God were not with him" (John 3:2). Jesus immediately challenges Nicodemus with conversation about the necessity of spiritual rebirth: "Very truly I tell you, no one can see the kingdom of God unless they are born again" (v. 3). This rebirth is a birth born of water and Spirit. Nicodemus is baffled yet intrigued about all of this. Jesus goes on to teach about the necessity of the Son of Man being lifted up in order for all who believe to have eternal life in him. In this encounter Jesus offers beautiful words: "For God so loved the world that he gave his one and only Son, that whoever believes in him shall not perish but have eternal life. For God did not send his Son into the world to condemn the world, but to save the world through him" (v. 16-17). Two things are quite important to recognize in the encounter with Nicodemus.

First, this is the rare occasion that a religious leader of the day comes with sincerity to ask Jesus about his teaching. The norm is for Pharisees, scribes, and priests to confront Jesus with questions meant to entrap him to give answers that will discredit him. They come as opponents. Nicodemus comes openly. Jesus responds to his openness with willingness to disclose what God is doing. There is a need for everyone to experience spiritual rebirth. This is the work of the Spirit. It is a work of grace and a work of love. The sacrifice of the Son of Man is necessary for this new beginning, an invitation to new life in the kingdom of God.

The second thing to note in this encounter is the true depth of God's graceful love Jesus is disclosing. Love has motivated the gift of God's Son, a gift necessary for eternal life to be realized. The coming of the Son is an act of salvation, not an act of condemnation and judgment. The world is not condemned by the coming of the Son; the world is saved by the coming of the Son. It is important to see this as the text clearly states; to avoid fitting the text into the neat box of evangelical Christianity as a propositional truth: if you believe, then you will be saved. This, of course, comes with the unspoken other side of the coin: if you do not believe, you will not be saved. But here Nicodemus is being taught that the coming of the Son is for rebirth into eternal life, an act of love and grace, not an act of judgment. The implications are huge: the world, the cosmos, will be saved through him.

On a Sabbath, a certain man born blind at birth catches the attention of the disciples. They have a reasonable curiosity and ask Jesus, "Rabbi, who sinned, this man or his parents, that he was born blind?" (John 9:2). "Neither this man nor his parents sinned," Jesus replies. "This happened so that the works of God might be displayed in him. As long as it is day, we must do the works of him who sent me. Night is coming, when no one can work. While I am in the world, I am the light of the world'" (vv. 3-5).

With saliva and mud, Jesus packs the man's eyes and instructs him to wash in the Pool of Siloam. With his blindness healed, the man tells his friends and neighbors that Jesus has restored his vision. The man who has begged for years in blindness is now giving witness to the healing power of Jesus. Already the leaders have decreed that anyone claiming Jesus to be the Messiah will be put out of the synagogue. The parents are afraid to respond to the Pharisees' requests concerning their son's healing. The witness of the man himself under their intense questioning infuriates the Pharisees as he answers, "Now that is remarkable! You don't know where he comes from, yet he opened my eyes. We know that God does not listen to sinners. He listens to the godly person who does his will. Nobody has ever heard of opening the eyes of a man born blind. If this man were not from God, he could do nothing" (John 9:30-33). They reply to him, "You were steeped in sin at birth; how dare you lecture us!" (v. 34).

After being cast out of the synagogue fellowship, the man is again in the presence of Jesus. He confesses his belief in the Son of Man and that Jesus is the special one sent from God. Jesus says, "For judgment I have come into this world, so that the blind will see and those who see will become blind" (John 9:39). The Pharisees wonder if Jesus is calling them blind, to which he replies, "If you were blind, you would not be guilty of sin; but now that you claim you can see, your guilt remains" (v. 41).

This encounter is an important one regarding a Jesus worldview. Whose fault is behind sickness and infirmity? Are parents to blame for defects in their children? Is illness or bad fortune a clear indication that there is sin in someone's life? We need to see that in this encounter Jesus is clear: a man born blind at birth does not indicate that his infirmity is a punishment for sin. The Pharisees do assign sin as the reason for the man's blindness; for them, a child born without eyesight is born "steeped in sin." Jesus sees things differently. The unfair hurts, infirmities, and disadvantages we encounter in life are not punishment for our sins. They are opportunities for us to experience God's grace, healing, and love in the midst of living with sickness and infirmity.

My father died quite young with cancer. He was fifty-three. A seminary neighbor meant well, I am sure, when he asked me to join a prayer circle that prayed for my dad's healing. It was not the first time I had asked God to heal Dad, and it would not be the last. But this time I was in a circle with persons who emphasized that he would definitely be healed if we had complete and total faith. After my father's death and I returned home from the funeral, my neighbor expressed his sympathy but also said, "I have to believe that somewhere along the line there was a lack of faith on someone's part that our prayers were not answered." In that moment I definitely felt like I was hearing a view of healing that simply did not resonate with me. Almost forty years later

I know why: My neighbor's worldview was much more like the Pharisees than like Jesus.

In his encounter with the blind man, Jesus warns us about assigning guilt and responsibility to others for the infirmities they or their loved ones may face. The guilt of persons who glibly interpret the suffering of others as a sign of God's punishment or judgment remains. Followers of Jesus should know better.

Seeing Jesus with His Opponents

Jesus encountered strong opposition from the onset to the conclusion of his earthly ministry. It is instructional to note who were the persistent critics and opponents of Christ and just how he handled encounters with them. The encounters of confrontation are persistent and numerous in the Gospels. A brief look at some of those episodes will help us as we ponder the worldview of Jesus in the face of opposition.

Early in Mark's gospel there is a criticism aimed at Jesus as he heals and teaches at Capernaum. We know the story of the friends who lower a paralytic man through an opening in the roof. Jesus sees their act of great faith and says to their friend, "Son, your sins are forgiven" (2:5). Teachers of the law are present and consider this blasphemy. Only God can forgive sins. Let us give them some grace here. They are right about only God forgiving sins. And, this is early in the ministry of Jesus. They have scant proof or evidence that Jesus is God in the flesh.

Jesus confronts their questioning. He tells the paralyzed man to rise and walk, and he does. But in conversation with his critics, Jesus is clear that his forgiving sins is not blasphemous, but legitimate. "But I want you to know that the Son of Man has authority on earth to forgive sins" (Mark 2:10). This will be the crux of the arguments between Jesus and the scribes and Pharisees. Their concerns are valid if Jesus is just a man with gifts of healing and teaching. But Jesus is vindicated by the authenticity of his claims—that he is the Son of Man, sent from God, doing the will of God.

Jesus has come to define blasphemy for himself as crediting God with what God did not say or do or refusing to acknowledge as authentic what God has actually said or done. If God is not in Jesus, leading Jesus to teach, heal, and eventually offer himself as a sacrifice, then the critics are right. Jesus is making a false claim. But if Jesus is right in his claims of oneness with the Father and obedience to God's mission, then woe to those who refuse to believe and accept his authenticity.

Throughout the Gospels, Jesus is criticized and rebuked for failing to follow the Law. Healing on the Sabbath, failing to fast, walking through a grain field on the Sabbath, touching the unclean, eating and drinking with sinners: all of these are legitimate complaints, unless—and this is the big exception— Jesus truly is anointed of God and one with the Father for this special ministry. If Jesus is indeed Lord of the Sabbath, these exceptions to recognized piety are legitimate.

This issue of rightful recognition of who Jesus really is comes to a head early on when Pharisees from Jerusalem come to see and hear Jesus. At the point in Mark's narrative that even his family believes Jesus is out of his mind, the teachers of the Law say, "He is possessed by Beelzebub! By the prince of demons, he is driving out demons" (3:22). Jesus replies:

How can Satan drive out Satan? If a kingdom is divided against itself, that kingdom cannot stand. If a house is divided against itself, that house cannot stand. And if Satan opposes himself and is divided, he cannot stand; his end has come. In fact, no one can enter a strong man's house without first tying him up. Then he can plunder the strong man's house. Truly, I tell you, people can be forgiven all their sins and every slander they utter, but whoever blasphemes against the Holy Spirit will never be forgiven; they are guilty of an eternal sin. (vv. 23-29)

The persistent unwillingness to recognize the authenticity of Jesus lasts until the end of his life. There is no more poignant moment in the trial of Jesus than when the high priest asks, "Are you the Messiah, the Son of the Blessed One?" (Mark 14:61). When Jesus answers, "I am," the high priest dramatically tears his clothes in anguish. This is the ultimate blasphemy in the eyes of Jesus' critics. This is what makes Jesus worthy of death in their eyes.

Jesus clearly calls out the scribes and Pharisees for their hypocrisy. Believing themselves righteous for their meticulous devotion to knowing and keeping the law, Jesus chides them for missing the whole point. Their failure to practice compassion and kindness clearly indicates to Jesus that they misunderstand God and God's intentions in giving the Law. By the end of his ministry Jesus is ready to confront them with a blistering address. Previously he has warned his followers about the "leaven of the Pharisees." Now he is exposing them in no uncertain terms.

"The teachers of the Law and the Pharisees sit in Moses' seat. So, you must be careful to do everything they tell you. But do not do what they do, for they do not practice what they preach" (Matt. 23:2-3). In a long discourse in the same chapter of Matthew's gospel, Jesus critiques the Pharisees: They put their burdens of conforming to the Law on the backs of others, weighty burdens they are unwilling to help others carry. They are showy in their piety. They love their status. They love the privilege their status affords them. Among the disciples they are to avoid giving one another titles of distinction. Then Jesus announces seven woes on the Pharisees:

1. They are eager to proselytize and then make their converts "twice as much a child of hell as you are" (v. 15).
2. They are blind guides making empty oaths before God (vv. 16-22).
3. They are strict tithers, yet "have neglected the more important matters of the law—justice, mercy, and faithfulness. You should have practiced the latter without neglecting the former" (v. 23).
4. They are pathetic in "straining at gnats" in some cases while "swallowing a camel" in others (v. 24).
5. They shine up their outside appearances, but inside "are full of greed and self-indulgence" (v. 25).
6. They are whitewashed tombs (v. 27).
7. They are snakes and vipers (v. 33).

In the act of cleansing the temple, recorded in Luke 19, Jesus enters Jerusalem clearly confronting the abuses of the religious leaders of his day. The chief priests, teachers of the law, and other leaders want to kill him. How does Jesus see these religious leaders in such a light that he vehemently opposes them? He sees their unbelief, their unwillingness to accept what God is doing in their midst. He sees their hypocrisy. He sees an outward piety that cannot atone for uncaring, unloving, and unforgiving hearts. He sees them tediously practice their religion of law-keeping and ritual and project their practices as demands on others. They are full of themselves and their self-righteousness. They are empty in spirit. They have made law-keeping so burdensome as to become silly. Yet, they have missed the most important aspects of God's intentions. These persons have willfully ignored the clarity of the prophet Micah's answer to the question of what God requires, "To act justly, and to love mercy and to walk humbly with your God" (Mic. 6:8).

Part of developing a Jesus worldview is to take seriously what Jesus opposed. Jesus could have taken on Caesar and the Romans as enemies. He could have focused his opposition on persons considered immoral or unclean. He could have focused his judgment on other religious notions, ideas, and practices that strayed from worship of the one true God. But the Pharisees and scribes, the religious legalists, were the focus of his opposition. They had distorted God's intent and were blind to God's will. They were unable to see the day of God's visitation and the inbreaking of God's kingdom. They were champions of external righteousness achieved by keeping law and custom. They were blind to God's heart, which is far more concerned with matters of justice and compassion. They were enemies of grace. And, Jesus opposed them. It is important for us to have eyes to see and hearts to understand.

Questions for Discussion/Reflection

1. What catches your attention when you look at the relationship between Jesus and his family? How well do you react to his broader view of family to include brothers and sisters who seek to do the will of God? How does Jesus' view of family challenge you?

2. In what ways do you believe the church is tempted in much the same way Jesus was tempted? How well do we resist these temptations?

3. How should Christians respond to children in ways that are consistent with how Jesus viewed children? What do you believe Jesus meant by saying that entrance into the kingdom of heaven requires that we must first become as children?

4. Do you see in Jesus an uncommon openness and compassion toward women? Is it fair to say that Jesus welcomed women into discipleship and valued their partnership in ministry?

5. Is a ministry of healing as central to you and your congregation as it was to the life and ministry of Jesus? Do we treat those with whom we minister with the same compassion Jesus showed?

6. It seems that often the goal of Jesus in healing was restoration. Persons considered unclean were made clean and could resume life with their family and religious community. Healing restored dignity and wholeness of life. Are our ministries of benevolence and care today as focused on the ultimate goal of restoration? When we care for the sick and the needy, do we also offer the gift of community?

7. As we listen to persons espousing Christian and biblical views and hear the things that anger and alarm them, does it seem that they are aligned with the example of Christ? How well have you done in aligning yourself to oppose what Jesus opposed?

CHAPTER 4

Seeing in His Teachings

The ministry life of Jesus focused on the development of his disciples; on healing and restoring the sick, blind, lame, and demon-possessed; and on teaching the multitudes. Time and again the reaction of the crowds to the teaching of Jesus was one of amazement. From his early temple encounter with the elders as a twelve-year-old right up through his teaching in the temple the week of his death, Jesus consistently astounded the multitudes and confounded his critics with a teaching so inspired and original that they were left saying, "We have never heard teaching like this."

To begin to see the world as Jesus saw the world, we need to carefully listen to his teaching. We need to listen with faith and pray for understanding. Jesus taught his followers through his teaching, especially with parables. For those who want to appropriate the teachings of Jesus in the center of their own worldview, Matthew 13:11-17 is important.

In this passage the disciples ask, "Why do you speak to the people in parables?" (v. 10). Jesus replies, "Because the knowledge of the secrets of the kingdom of heaven has been given to you, but not to them" (v. 11), referencing the story of the call of Isaiah to a ministry where persons, "though seeing, they do not see; though hearing they do not hear or understand" (v. 13). The disciples are blessed to be able both to hear and understand Jesus' teaching. "But blessed are your eyes because they see, and your ears because they hear. For truly I tell you, many prophets and righteous people longed to see what you see but did not see it, and to hear what you hear but did not hear it" (vv. 16-17).

As we look at the teachings of Jesus, may God grant us the insight to see what Jesus was really seeing and to hear what Jesus was really saying. We should all recognize that throughout the history of the church not every claim of consistency with the teachings of Jesus has been valid; not every worldview put forth as a Christian worldview is rightly aligned with the teaching of Christ. With humility we ask of God to hear, see, and understand the teachings of Jesus so that we might rightly align our lives with all he taught.

Seeing in His Priorities

Luke 4 tells us of Jesus' visit to his hometown synagogue in the early days of his earthly ministry. At the synagogue he reads from the scroll of the prophet Isaiah: "The Spirit of the Lord is on me, because he has anointed me to proclaim good news to the poor. He has sent me to proclaim freedom for the prisoners and recovery of sight to the blind, to set the oppressed free, to proclaim the year of the Lord's favor" (vv. 18-19). After reading this passage Jesus shocks his hometown friends with these words: "Today this scripture is fulfilled in your hearing" (v. 21).

Jesus wants these words from Isaiah to clarify the purpose of his coming and the focus of his ministry. These prophetic words of promised emancipation and redemption become the guiding star he follows: he is to proclaim good news to the poor and freedom to prisoners, give sight to the blind, set the oppressed free from their bondage, and declare the good news of God's jubilee to all who yearn to hear of it.

Claims to represent a Christian worldview apart from taking seriously this early identification of the purpose of Jesus' ministry are invalid. Jesus cared for the poor and their plight. He stood with the oppressed and even the imprisoned—he desired to set them free from their bondage. He cared for the sick and the hurting; he wanted to bring sight to the blind. He believed in the principles of jubilee, when debts are forgiven and land is restored to the people. Any unwillingness to embrace concern for the very people Jesus cared for and ministered to is a rejection of his teaching. A Jesus worldview embraces concerns for the poor, oppressed, sick, and wounded.

On the other end of his ministry Jesus makes the same points in his telling story of the judgment of the nations. In Matthew 25 we learn that "when the Son of Man comes in his glory, and all the angels with him, he will sit on his glorious throne. All the nations will be gathered before him, and he will separate the people from one another as a shepherd separates the sheep from the goats" (vv. 31-32).

How will this judgment be carried out? By what criteria will the nations be judged?

"Then the King will say to those on his right, 'Come, you who are blessed by my Father; take your inheritance, the kingdom prepared for you since the creation of the world. For I was hungry and you gave me something to eat,

I was thirsty and you gave me something to drink, I was a stranger and you invited me in, I needed clothes and you clothed me, I was sick and you looked after me, I was in prison and you came to visit me'" (Matt. 25:34-36). The ones judged righteous are pleased with the judgment they receive. But they are also surprised. "Lord, when did we see you hungry and feed you, or thirsty and give you something to drink? When did we see you a stranger and invite you in, or needing clothes and clothe you? When did we see you sick or in prison and go to visit you?" (vv. 37-38). Jesus replies that the king will say to the righteous, "Truly I tell you, whatever you did for one of the least of these brothers and sisters of mine, you did for me" (v. 40).

The nations judged to be guilty are the ones who neglect to do the things the righteous do. The unrighteous do not visit the sick and imprisoned nor give food and drink to the hungry and thirsty. They do not welcome the stranger nor clothe those in need. This harsh judgment comes as a surprise; the wicked will argue that they never saw Jesus in any of those conditions and neglected his need. But Jesus will indict them, saying, "Truly I tell you, whenever you did not do for one of the least of these, you did not do for me" (25:45). The judgment is announced: "Then they will go away to eternal punishment, but the righteous to eternal life" (v. 46).

Although this is a judgment of the nations, I would not argue that this passage has no personal implications for the follower of Jesus. A disciple should hear these words and act on them. We should recognize the personal need to see Christ in others, especially in the hungry, poor, needy, oppressed, and unwelcomed. But recognition is not the standard of judgment in this teaching; it is action. As individual followers of Jesus we should give food and drink, welcome, clothe, and visit. But again, this passage is unique in its assertion that this is how the nations will ultimately be judged.

If one is to inject a Jesus worldview into political discussions about national policies and behaviors, it seems this is the place to start. Jesus clearly taught us that nations will be judged by how they treat the hungry, thirsty, stranger, homeless, imprisoned, and needy. Proponents of a biblical or Christian worldview that endorses a political agenda that ignores the plight of those dear to the heart of Christ should be challenged. We may have differences of opinion on the best way as a people to address these problems, but to ignore these issues is to ignore the teaching of Jesus.

If we take seriously the goal of living with a Jesus worldview, we should take seriously the answer Jesus gave to anyone asking him for his highest priority. The Gospels share just such a moment with us:

> One of them, an expert in the law, tested him with this question, "Teacher, which is the greatest commandment in the Law?" Jesus replied, "Love the Lord your God with all your heart and with all your soul and with all your mind. This is the first and greatest commandment. And the second is like it: Love your neighbor as yourself. All the Law and the Prophets hang on these two commandments." (Matt. 22:35-40)

What did Jesus believe to be the most important instruction from God, the supreme commandment? He believed it was to love. First, we must love God wholeheartedly, with all of our being, with every aspect of ourselves. We are to love God and hold nothing of ourselves back in extending that love. This was the Old Testament command that the Jews prayed daily, the *shema* of Israel. But there was a second commandment from the Old Testament that Jesus elevated to be of equal importance to loving God.

We must love our neighbor as we love ourselves. We cannot live selfishly and live consistently with the teachings of Jesus. No matter how piously we display a love for God, it is worth little if we are unwilling to love our neighbors. The question follows, "Just who is my neighbor?" Luke puts this question on the lips of a teacher of the Law after hearing Christ speak to the subject of the greatest commandment and what one must do to inherit eternal life. Jesus replies with the story of the Good Samaritan, found in Luke 10:33-37.

A man traveling to Jericho is beaten by robbers and left for dead beside the road. A priest and a Levite pass the poor fellow by. But a Samaritan comes to where the man is and takes pity on him, proceeding to bandage his wounds and pour on oil and wine. Then the Samaritan puts the wounded man on his own donkey and takes him to an inn where he gives the innkeeper money for the man's care and promises on his return to repay the innkeeper for any uncovered expenses. Jesus asks of the expert in the law, "Which one of these three do you think was a neighbor to the man who fell into the hands of robbers?" The man can only answer the obvious: "The one who had mercy on him." Jesus simply instructs him: "Go and do likewise."

Love God and love your neighbor. In the broadest of terms, our neighbor is not just the person living next door. Our neighbor is not confined to our kin and friends. Loving a neighbor requires action—acts of compassion and mercy. A Jesus worldview embraces the challenge to love God above all other loves and to love God with all of our being. And, a Jesus worldview commits to the challenge to love neighbor as self, with a love that is broad and inclusive, sacrificial and compassionate. A Jesus worldview must not neglect or even diminish the importance of his clear answer to the question, "What is the greatest commandment?"

In an attempt to articulate a compelling vision to guide us from 2015 to 2020, my congregation engaged in a wonderful process of discovering and defining our vision. The resulting document of our work together is lengthy and filled with steps to take in implementing the vision, but the vision itself is simple and clear. We asked ourselves, "Why do we exist as a church?" The answer: we exist to love our God. We have sung a beautiful Mark Hayes chorus repeatedly these past few years:

To love our God, the reason we live;
To love our God, the highest call.
Nothing satisfies our soul,
gives life meaning,
makes us whole.
For this purpose we were made:
to love our God.

Another image/chorus has also guided us. Yes, we exist to love our God, but we also exist to love our neighbor. Borrowing from the rich imagery of Psalm 1, we see our congregation in the midst of our small town "like a tree planted by streams of water, which yields its fruit in season and whose leaf does not whither" (v. 3). We hope our tree provides shade and refuge to our community. We want its branches to be inclusive and inviting. We want to bear the fruit of relevant and significant ministry; to see the poor and the needy, the hungry and the thirsty, the stranger and the neglected and to love them as neighbor. It is a compelling and challenging vision that has captured our imagination and attention. We sing a second chorus, whose composer we have not been able to discover:

> We are like a tree planted by the river.
> Its leaf never withers,
> for it grows in the deepest sod.
> Sturdy and strong, for secure is its root,
> and in due season, it sends forth its fruit.
> We are like a tree planted by the river
> that flows from the throne room of God.

Like a tree firmly planted . . . to love our God! This has been our congregation's sustaining vision the last half of this decade. We exist to love God and love our neighbor. That is what Jesus taught.

Seeing in His Parables

Jesus taught in parables, or simple stories that instill a lesson and contain moral content. Jesus believed a parable could provide insight to a person with "ears to hear," while that same parable might confound the person who lacks those same "ears to hear." The mysteries of God's kingdom could be shared with his disciples as he taught them in parables. Those parables are numerous. But let's look at some key ones that address themes important to constructing a Jesus worldview.

The Parable of the Sower, found in Mark 4:3-8, occupies an important role in the teachings of Jesus:

> Listen, a farmer went out to sow his seed. As he was scattering the seed, some fell along the path, and the birds came and ate it up. Some fell on rocky places, where it did not have much soil. It sprang up quickly because the soil was shallow. But when the sun came up, the plants were scorched, and they withered because they had no root. Other seed fell among thorns, which grew up and choked the plants, so that they did not bear grain. Still other seed fell on good soil. It came up, grew and produced a crop, some multiplying thirty, some sixty, some a hundred times.

The preaching of God's kingdom is a sowing of seed. Not all will take root, but the seed is sown generously. The opportunity to receive the kingdom's good news is shared with all. But only where the seed falls in good soil will it take root and thrive until harvest. The yield of the harvest varies, but there will be growth that leads to harvest wherever the kingdom is received in "good soil."

This parable is told by the gospel writers Matthew, Mark, and Luke with accompanying explanation of the various types of soil to follow. Satan can snatch some seed off of rocky soil. Some people joyfully receive the seed but never put down the roots necessary for growth. Persecution will cause some to fall away. The worries of the world will choke out kingdom growth in others. But where the soil is good, the harvest will be good. The kingdom will take hold, and lives will bear good fruit.

In other parables Jesus continues to use the metaphor of sowing seed for the kingdom of God. The one who sows the seed sleeps at night and cannot explain how and why the seed grows as it does. But he can certainly see the growth and recognize the time for the harvest (Mark 4:26-29). The kingdom is like a mustard seed, small when it is sown, but large and inviting when it grows to maturity (Mark 4:30-32). Should the tares sown by "the enemy" be a reason to plow under the whole field? No, the parable encourages letting the wheat from the good seed and the tares grow together until harvest (Matt. 13:24-29).

Jesus told several parables about servants in the kingdom of God. Some are identified as wicked and therefore receive judgment. Some are praised for their devotion, responsibility, and even ingenuity. The parable of the talents is one of those well-known tales.

A man on a journey entrusts wealth to his servants, with differing amounts reflecting differences in their abilities. The ones given five or two talents both double the amount they receive and are able to show the owner a marvelous return on investment when he returns. Alas, the one-talent servant fears the owner and simply hides his one talent, his one bag of money, in the ground. His unwillingness to invest and increase what he was given angers the master: "You wicked, lazy servant! So you knew that I harvest where I have not sown and gather where I have not scattered seed? Well then, you should have put my money on deposit with the bankers, so that when I returned I would have received it back with interest" (Matt. 25:26-27). This servant is deemed worthless. His one talent is taken from him and given to the servant who has turned five into ten. And, the worthless slave is cast out into a place of "weeping and gnashing of teeth."

God invests the kingdom in us. It is a stewardship, a trust. Inspired, we are to invest what we have in service to others. God desires to find us using our gifts, talents, and opportunities wisely. Life is not about accumulating wealth. The one who tears down his barns to build bigger barns in order to live a life of luxury is condemned: "You fool! This very night your life will be demanded from you. Then who will get what you have prepared for yourself?" (Luke 12:20). To store up for oneself without being rich toward God is a foolish way to live.

In another parable a shrewd servant is commended for his quick thinking. When his master requires an accounting of his stewardship, the manager knows he will be fired for his waste. So, he decides he will make friends who will help him when he is out of a job. He fraudulently reduces the amounts owed by his master's debtors, winning their appreciation. Surprisingly, his master is impressed at his opportunistic thinking. The real point Jesus makes is this: "Use worldly wealth for yourself to gain friends for yourselves, so that when it is gone, you will be welcomed into eternal dwellings" (Luke 16:9).

Wealth is not our goal. It can be used as a means to an end. But God demands that we live for a larger purpose than wealth accumulation. A Jesus worldview needs to take seriously his succinct summary after telling the parable of the shrewd servant, "You cannot serve both God and money" (Luke 16:13).

In Matthew 18:32-34, Jesus teaches that someone who receives grace and forgiveness should be willing to extend the same to others. In this parable, a servant owes his king ten thousand bags of gold. Unable to pay, he and his family are ordered into servitude. The man begs for mercy, and it is granted. No sooner does he receive such magnanimous grace than he goes out and demands repayment from someone who owes him a hundred silver coins. He turns a deaf ear to his debtor's plea for mercy, and has him thrown into jail for the unpaid debt. When the news gets back to the man's master, the servant is judged with severity: "You wicked servant, I canceled all that debt of yours because you begged me to. Shouldn't you have had mercy on your fellow servant just as I had on you?" In anger the master hands the servant over to the jailers to be tortured, until he can pay back all he owes.

Jesus sees God as forgiving us all the greatest of debts in the forgiveness of our sins. In turn, we are to be forgiving of others, always ready to extend grace.

The stewardship of the servant requires a certain readiness. No one knows when the master will return. No one can anticipate when a time of accounting is required. Jesus calls for readiness: "Therefore keep watch because you do not know when the owner of the house will come back—whether in the evening, or at midnight, or when the rooster crows, or at dawn. If he comes suddenly do not let him find you sleeping. What I say to you I say to everyone, 'Watch!'" (Mark 13:35-37).

The greatest judgment of all falls on the servants who will not receive those sent from the landowner of the vineyard. They seize three servants sent to collect his fruit: one is beaten, a second killed, a third stoned to death. His last hope is to send his son. Surely, they will not mistreat him. In fact, they conspire together: "This is the heir. Come, let's kill him and take his inheritance." So, they take him and throw him out of the vineyard and kill him (Matt. 21:38-39). An obvious foreshadowing of those who will reject him and kill him, Jesus is revealing the depth of evil within those who oppose God's redemptive work.

The idea of being ready for God's appearing is reinforced in other parables. The ten virgins need to be prepared for the wedding feast with oil in their lamps (Matt. 25:1-13). The guest without the proper wedding attire is thrown out of the wedding banquet (Matt. 22:1-14).

A true Jesus worldview has a sense of being present in the kingdom of God, fully aware, fully prepared. An invitation to life in God's kingdom is urgent. It cannot be delayed or postponed. It calls us to live obediently now.

Other parables describe the kingdom in terms of a banquet. A certain man hosts a banquet, inviting many guests. The regrets pour in, accompanied by excuses: "I need to check out the new land I bought." "I need to try out the five oxen I purchased." "I am a newlywed; count me out." Undeterred, the host instructs his servant to widen the invitation: "Go out quickly into the streets and alleys of the town and bring in the poor, the crippled, the blind, and the lame" (Luke 14:21). The obedient servant follows instructions. Many new guests arrive, but still there is room at the table. The master widens the invitation yet again: "Go out to the roads and country lanes and compel them to come in, so that my house will be full" (v. 23).

This is a beautiful depiction of God's banquet table. The religious—the righteous—are certainly invited, but they are the very ones most likely to excuse themselves from the party. The invitation extends to everyone—God wants his house and table full. All are invited. No one is left out.

In another parable about who has a seat at the Lord's table, a certain rich man enjoys his own earthly banquets on a regular basis. Every day he dresses up and dines lavishly. Outside his gate is a beggar names Lazarus. After the meals are done, Lazarus joins the dogs in scrounging crumbs fallen from the table. The dogs lick his open wounds. Then, both men die.

Jesus describes the afterlife the two men experience in a very Jewish way. The unrighteous and the righteous have all gone to a place where they can see and hear each other, but with two very different ways of living. The unnamed rich man is tormented in Hades; Lazarus is comforted at the side of Abraham. No better depiction of the spirit and attitude of one consigned to Hades could be given than what the rich man asks: "Father Abraham, have pity on me and send Lazarus to dip the tip of his finger in water, and cool my tongue, because I am in agony in this fire" (Luke 16:24). Imagine the self-centered gall of this rich man. Having ignored Lazarus' plight, competing with the dogs for table crumbs, now he wants Lazarus to comfort him. He makes no plea for mercy; he does not ask to be rescued from the place of torment. But he would gladly rob Lazarus of his reward and send him to Hades just to cool his tongue and soothe his agony.

Abraham replies, "Son, remember that in your lifetime you received good things, while Lazarus received bad things, but now he is comforted here and you are in agony. And besides all this, between us and you a great chasm has been set in place, so that those who want to go from here to you cannot, nor can anyone cross over from there to us" (Luke 16:25-26). Even the rich man's request that someone be sent to warn his brothers is denied; they have the Law and the Prophets. The lack of repentance does not come from ignorance; it is the result of a hardened heart.

The contrast between the righteous and unrighteous is also clear in a parable told in Luke 18:10-14. A Pharisee and a tax collector go to the temple to pray. The Pharisee stands by himself and prays, "God, I thank you that I am not like other people—robbers, evildoers, adulterers—or even like this tax collector. I fast twice a week and give a tenth of all I get." But the tax collector stands at a distance and will not even look up to heaven. He beats his breast and pleads, "God, have mercy on me a sinner." At the end of his story, Jesus comments: "I tell you, this man, rather than the other, went home justified before God."

Jesus makes sure we understand the value of the kingdom, a value unsurpassed by anything else. It is the treasure hid in a field, worth selling all one has just to buy that field. It is the amazing pearl that will cause a merchant to sell all he has to possess that remarkable pearl (Matt. 13:44-46). And, the kingdom of God celebrates the worth of the individual. God seeks to find, to redeem, to return anyone who is lost. The return of the one lost sheep is celebrated; even though ninety-nine remain secure in the fold (Luke 15:3-7). When sweeping at night leads a woman to find her lost coin, she calls her friends and neighbors to rejoice with her (Luke 15:8-10). And, when an ungrateful and irresponsible young son has squandered everything and returns home humbled, his return is celebrated by a forgiving father.

This son is clothed with a robe and a ring and sandals, and treated to a party with a fatted calf to eat and musicians to play. The older, faithful son is unwilling to join the party. He cannot understand a father who so quickly forgives. It all seems to violate a sense of fairness. But his father explains, "You are always with me, and everything I have is yours. But we had to celebrate and be glad, because this brother of yours was dead and is alive again; he was lost and is found" (Luke 15:31-32).

Seeing in His Sayings

Apart from parables, Jesus said simple but important things that should shape a Jesus worldview. Some are quite obscure, for example: "To what shall I compare this generation? They are like children sitting in the marketplaces and calling out to others, 'We played the pipe for you, and you did not dance; we sang a dirge and you did not mourn'" (Matt. 11:16-17).

Jesus has grown weary of his critics. They criticized John the Baptist for his eccentricities and considered him demon-possessed. They have criticized Jesus for being a glutton and drunkard and hanging out with the wrong crowd. And so, he uses the illustration of children playing in the marketplaces: They want to play weddings, but the others won't dance. They want to play funerals, but the others won't mourn.

Jesus invites us to embrace life, to dance and to mourn. There is no virtue in being a sideline critic or a passive-aggressive complainer. Get in the game! Dance the dance! Sing the dirge!

Jesus speaks words of both invitation and comfort when he says, "Come to me, all you who are weary and burdened, and I will give you rest. Take my yoke upon you and learn from me, for I am gentle and humble in heart, and you will find rest for your souls. For my yoke is easy and my burden is light" (Matt. 11:28-30). To the weary Jesus offers rest. There are still loads to carry and burdens to bear, but Jesus makes the paths easier to navigate and the burdens lighter to bear. The yoke of discipleship attaches us to the right way to live as a follower of Jesus.

Jesus insists on emphasizing the high cost of discipleship: "Foxes have dens and birds have nests, but the Son of Man has no place to lay his head" (Luke 9:58). "Let the dead bury their own dead, but you go and proclaim the kingdom of God" (v. 60). "No one who puts a hand to the plow and looks back is fit for service in the kingdom of God" (v. 62). But Jesus holds himself to the highest demands of serving God. He consistently teaches of both the inevitability and necessity of his own suffering and death:

> The hour has come for the Son of Man to be glorified. Very truly I tell you, unless a kernel of wheat falls to the ground and dies, it remains only a single seed. But if it dies, it produces many seeds. Anyone who loves their life will lose it, while anyone who hates their life in this world will keep it for eternal life. Whoever serves me must follow me. (John 12:23-26)

There is no cheap grace to be found in the teaching of Jesus. There is a price to be paid for authentic discipleship. But no one stands more willing to lay down his own life sacrificially than Jesus.

Jesus teaches the crowds, "Listen to me, everyone, and understand this. Nothing outside a person can defile them by going into them. Rather, it is what comes out of a person that defiles them" (Mark 7:14-15). His words surely resonate with Paul's insistence that keeping dietary laws as prescribed in the Old Testament is not required of followers of Christ, particularly Gentile Christians. A strict, outward conformity to law and custom is not the goal of discipleship. The greater concern is what comes out of us—our words and actions. This is where Jesus clearly places his emphasis.

At several points Jesus challenges those, especially the religious leaders, who ask him for a sign, a verification of his ministry—even though his ministry has included one miraculous sign after another: the lame walk, the blind regain sight, the lepers are cleansed, the deaf can hear, the demon-possessed are calmed, and even those supposed dead are returned to life. In response to the Pharisees' request for a sign, Jesus replies: "A wicked and adulterous generation asks for a sign! But none will be given it except the sign of the prophet Jonah" (Matt. 12:39). His resurrection will be the sign of the authenticity of his ministry. No other signs will be given to engender belief. Their generation has had plenty of signs and warnings they were unwilling to heed.

An interesting point of note is Jesus' response to his disciples when they report someone driving out demons in his name, without being a part of the circle of followers. John informs Jesus, "We told him to stop, because he was not one of us" (Mark 9:38). Jesus replies that they should not try to stop the one healing in his name, "For no one who does a miracle in my name can in the next moment say anything bad about me, for whoever is not against us is for us" (vv. 39-40). Jesus does not insist that everyone else's ministry come under his direct authority; he can affirm the good work done by someone outside his inner circle.

In the Gospel of John, we find Jesus using images to reveal his true identity and purpose. These images are introduced with "I am."

- "I am the bread of life" (6:35).
- "I am the light of the world" (8:12).
- "I am the gate for the sheep" (10:7).
- "I am the good shepherd" (10:11).
- "I am the resurrection and the life" (11:25).

Jesus is the one who can satisfy our deepest hungers. His followers will walk in light, not darkness. He knows the sheep and cares for them; he is their entrance into the fold. The one who will live in Christ will live beyond death. In these statements Jesus pictures his followers in a dynamic and organic relationship with him. The disciples are connected with Christ. Jesus is the very source of their life—their bread, their light, their shepherd, their hope.

Seeing in His Passages of Judgment

I must confess that my own understanding of Jesus is more focused on his love. The gentle shepherd, the healing ambassador of God, the patient teacher, the person of inclusion and invitation, the willing sacrifice: these images are dominant in my own perception of Jesus. They are certainly biblical, authentic pictures of Jesus. But to ignore the righteous anger of Jesus or the hard teachings related to God's judgment is to miss significant insight into the worldview of Jesus. Earlier in this work we chronicled the encounters of Jesus with his critics, mainly the scribes and Pharisees. His words of judgment toward them were sharp and incisive.

The Synoptic Gospels all have significant passages near the end of Jesus' earthly ministry that speak of the coming "day of the Lord." These passages are typical of Jewish apocalyptic literature, dramatic passages that unveil a future time of judgment. The depiction of these coming days can be found in Matthew 24, Mark 13, and Luke 21. It is important to keep in mind the historical context as we interpret these texts.

In 70 AD the Roman siege of Jerusalem occurred. The temple was destroyed, and Jews were resettled in the Diaspora. That Jesus was speaking about this coming time of trial and destruction is the most logical interpretation. Note the remarks made by the disciples that prompted this apocalyptic discourse. As they are remarking how the temple is adorned with beautiful stones and with gifts dedicated to God, Jesus tells them: "As for what you see here, the time will come when no stone will be left on another, every one of them will be thrown down." The disciples ask their teacher, "When will these things happen? And what will be the sign that they are about to take place?'" (Luke 21:5-7). All that follows will be directly related to the disciples' questions about what will take place. To place these words of Jesus into a millennial scheme without taking seriously the first-century context misses the point. The Synoptics were all written just before or relatively soon after the events of 70 AD. The fall of Jerusalem and destruction of the temple no doubt weighed heavily on the minds of the gospel writers.

In the Gospels, Jesus describes this time of judgment with frightening, sobering words. Those who claim the time is here are deceivers. Wars and uprisings are not the sign that this apocalyptic event is ready to unfold. "Nation will rise against nation, and kingdom against kingdom. There will be great earthquakes, famines and pestilence in various places, and fearful events and great signs from heaven. But before all this, they will seize you and persecute you. They will hand you over to the synagogues and put you in prison, and you will be brought before kings and governors, and all on account of my name" (Luke 21:10-12). (The Book of Acts and the letters of Paul will later describe these things as, in fact, occurring.)

There is no teaching here that followers of Jesus will be taken away before persecution comes; indeed, they are warned to expect persecution. This will take place at a time when the synagogues remain viable, for the followers of Jesus will be subject to trial in them. Jesus promises to give his followers the words to say when the need for defense arises. But he warns that they can expect betrayal from their family and friends; they can expect to be the objects of hatred; they can expect that some of them will be martyred. But Jesus promises that those who persevere to the end will be rewarded: "But not a hair of your head will perish. Stand firm, and you will win life" (Luke 21:18-19).

They will know the dreadful day is near when the besieging armies are on the horizon. It will be time to seek refuge in the hills, to flee the cities. This historical act is to be seen as an act of judgment: "For this is a time of punishment in fulfillment of all that has been written" (Luke 21:22). The siege will be dreadful to endure. The vulnerable pregnant women and nursing mothers are to be pitied. It will be a day of distress, a day of wrath. "They will fall by the sword and will be taken as prisoners to all the nations. Jerusalem will be trampled on by the Gentiles until the times of the Gentiles are fulfilled" (v. 24).

A few details from Matthew's gospel add to our understanding of this apocalyptic vision. The disciples are encouraged to remain steadfast to the end: "But the one who stands firm to the end will be saved. And this gospel of the kingdom will be preached in the whole world as a testimony to all nations, and then the end will come" (Matt. 24:13-14). Both Matthew and Mark reference an apocalyptic image from Daniel, the "abomination that causes desolation," that most likely refers to the desecration of the temple.

The creation and the nations will quiver at the horrors of this coming day. Then the Son of Man will appear. "At that time they will see the Son of Man coming in a cloud with power and great glory. When these things begin to take place, stand up and lift up your heads, because your redemption is drawing near" (Luke 21:27-28). The only way this day of judgment may be brought to an end is through an act of God, the appearing of the Son of Man. When all of this will take place is not knowable; not even the Son of Man knows the date or hour. Jesus tells his followers that these things will happen before their generation is completely gone, once again reinforcing the idea that these texts are speaking of the coming fall of Jerusalem. The proper reaction to hearing this prediction of the coming day of judgment is to be ready, to stay aware. "Be always on the watch, and pray that you may be able to escape all that is about to happen, and that you may be able to stand before the Son of Man" (v. 36).

The coming day of judgment brings sadness, not delight, to the heart of Jesus. As he enters Jerusalem on the last Passover week of his earthly life and ministry, he weeps over it and says,

> If you, even you, had only known on this day what would bring you peace—but now it is hidden from your eyes. The days will come upon you when your enemies will build an embankment against you and encircle you and hem you in on every side. They will dash you to the ground, you and the children within your walls. They will not leave one stone on another, because you did not recognize the time of God's coming to you. (Luke 19:41-44)

During his ministry, Jesus had expressed anger toward those whom he believed had perverted God's intentions with their legalism, exclusivity, and self-righteousness. He overthrew the tables of money changers in the temple. He told parables of persons who received God's judgment. He warned of the coming dreadful, awful day of judgment. His words are steeped in tradition, especially the apocalyptic tradition of the Jews.

Evil will not go unpunished forever. Eventually a day of judgment falls. Those days are not outside of God's will or providence. They must be endured. They are filled with things that are fearful. But the people of God are called to persevere. And, ultimately redemption comes from God's appearing.

This understanding of the day of the Lord permeated Jewish apocalyptic literature. The people of God had experienced these awful days of judgment before—with attacks from Assyria, Babylon, and the Seleucids. They would see this new day of which Jesus spoke come to fruition at the hands of the

Romans. The New Testament Apocalypse of John would speak of another day yet to come, using similar language and imagery, quite likely referencing later persecution of the church by Rome.

Were the words of judgment spoken by Jesus only relevant to the historical situation of his day? I think not. While I would insist that we understand these texts best when we take seriously their first-century context, Jesus' teachings on judgment are relevant in constructing a Jesus worldview. I believe Jesus taught that a day of judgment awaits prolonged evil. When that time occurs, it is accompanied by great suffering. Religious leaders, political leaders, even nations, are accountable for their actions. The day of the Lord sheds light on evil and thwarts it. For those who seek to be true to God and to follow Jesus, they are not exempt from the suffering the day of judgment may bring. They are called to endure, but they also are given hope. Keep looking up. Redemption is on the way. The Son of Man will appear.

Questions for Discussion/Reflection

1. Do you agree that Jesus was decidedly concerned for the plight of the poor, the sick, and the oppressed? How well do you believe Christian individuals and congregations do in embracing his priority?

2. Are voices that claim to be Christian voices consistent with the teachings of Jesus on how the nations will be judged? How can we contribute to our nation taking seriously the teachings of Jesus concerning judgment and accountability?

3. Consider how Jesus answered the question regarding the greatest commandment. Do we simplify things too much when we assert that the highest purpose of Christians is to love?

4. How can we best apply the story of the Samaritan neighbor to our own lives? What are the implications of the story on how we treat others?

5. What parable most influences your understanding of Jesus' worldview? Why did you choose that parable? What parable of Jesus is most troubling for you, and why?

6. How do the parables influence your understanding of the kingdom of God, reflecting on what the parables ask of us as we live in the world and what the parables teach us about judgment and grace after life on earth has ended?

7. What is a saying of Jesus that you love? What saying of Jesus troubles you? What saying of Jesus comforts you?

8. Describe your thoughts on how Jesus spoke of judgment. How do the teachings of Jesus challenge some of the Christian assumptions we hear about salvation?

CHAPTER 5

Seeing in the Upper Room

Five of the twenty-one chapters in the Gospel of John record what took place while the disciples were in the upper room celebrating the Passover and their continuing conversation as they left the room just prior to Jesus' arrest, trial, and crucifixion. Much like Matthew introduces the ministry of Jesus in his gospel with the sermonic collection we know as the Sermon on the Mount, John emphasizes the teaching of Jesus shared with his disciples in the upper room and on the way to his arrest. I have heard John 13–17 called the best instruction in spiritual formation to be found in Scripture. In these poignant moments so close to his passion, Jesus reveals things to his disciples that are central to his worldview.

The Towel and Basin

The scene is set. Jesus knows the end is near. He will soon be leaving the world and his disciples. The powerful emotion he feels is love: "Having loved his own who were in the world, he loved them to the end" (John 13:1). Had the disciples been dining in the home of a wealthy host, it is likely that the guests would have been greeted by servants charged with the task of washing their feet. John tells us their meal is already in progress. Judas Iscariot is poised to carry out his betrayal of Jesus. Jesus is ready to model something of great importance to his disciples.

One can imagine the conflicting emotions the disciples feel. To have one's feet washed in cool water and toweled dry feels good. It is a luxury. Yet, it seems awkward that Jesus is taking on the role of servant and washing their feet. We are not surprised that impetuous Peter is the first to speak. He does not want Jesus to wash his feet. He believes it is just not right, but Jesus insists. So, Peter decides to opt for a larger bath. Jesus can go ahead and wash his hands and head. Jesus declines. The foot washing will be enough.

In a moment we realize that this act is about teaching and modeling. "Do you understand what I have done for you?" Jesus asks his disciples.

You call me "Teacher" and "Lord" and rightly so, for that is what I am. Now that I, your Lord and teacher, have washed your feet, you also should wash one another's feet. I have set you an example that you should do as I have done for you. Very truly I tell you, no servant is greater than his master, nor is a messenger greater than the one who sent him. Now that you know these things, you will be blessed if you do them. (John 13:12-17)

We have heard it said, "A picture is worth a thousand words." The picture of Jesus, stripped of his outer garments, bathing the feet of his disciples, is an image that should be central to any Jesus worldview. This one sent from God is not too good to perform a servant's task for those he loves. In this act he is sending a message central to his convictions. We are to serve others. And, his disciples, his followers, are to find their own towel and basin and wash someone else's feet. We are not above Jesus. If Jesus is a foot washer, we are to be foot washers.

The most prominent models of Christian ministers in our culture tend to be preachers and teachers, particularly those of some celebrity status. Seldom are these persons of prominence viewed as servants. In our churches we argue over who has legitimate claims to authority and who should be elevated to ordained positions. We compete for titles and offices and authority. But there is seldom a crowd competing for the towel and basin.

If our models of ministry do not call to mind images of service, then our models are wrong. I believe this is why Mother Teresa captured our hearts in the late twentieth century. With all of the celebrity ministers who seemed to be anything but feet-washing servants, we discovered a petite lady in Calcutta, India bathing the wounds of the sick. We saw a picture of a Christian leader who looked a lot like Jesus, washing feet. Ministry is about service. Followers of Jesus serve one another. The picture of Jesus washing feet in the upper room says so much. It should inform the way we view ministry and the way we view the world.

The New Commandment

After telling his disciples the disturbing news that one of them will betray him, and after Judas leaves the room to carry out his act of betrayal, Jesus is ready to give the disciples a new commandment to guide them. As Moses gave the law to the Old Testament people of God, now Jesus is ready to share a new law with his disciples.

"A new command I give you. Love one another. As I have loved you, so you must love one another. By this everyone will know that you are my disciples, if you love one another" (John 13:34-35). No ten commandments are needed this time, just one—love. But how hard this commandment is to keep!

We could keep this new commandment of Jesus if all he asks for is an assent to the idea that we know we ought to love one another. As long as we can piously say, "I know we are supposed to love everyone, but that does not mean we have to like everyone," we can exist with the new commandment. But Jesus is asking us to love one another supremely; to love as he loves.

We are called to love one another with a sacrificial, giving, servant love. And, knowing Jesus, we can only imagine how wide his idea of "one another" must be. It surely includes more than family, neighbors, and friends, and even more than sisters and brothers in our congregation. It would be just like Jesus not only to ask us to love one another, but also to include in his definition of "one another" those folks who are quite different from ourselves, persons we find not so easy to love.

Jesus even says that this is how we will be rightly and correctly known as his followers—authentic followers of Christ. The degree to which we obey the new command to love one another is the degree to which we are recognized as disciples of Jesus. "And they'll know we are Christians by our love, by our love, yes, they'll know we are Christians by our love." This chorus was not too hard to sing when I was a young Christian, but it has been much harder to live out through my many years of attempting to follow Jesus.

The new commandment makes the disciples—and us—uncomfortable. To break the tension in the upper room, Peter speaks up, asking, "Lord where are you going?" (John 13:36). Interestingly, he does not want to talk with Jesus about the new commandment. He does not ask Jesus to elaborate; to teach them more about the best way to love one another. Peter prefers to change the subject. (He was not the last to do this. Throughout the ages, people have deflected from the commandment to love one another to focus instead on some other pressing matter of ministry or theology. We are uncomfortable with the bold simplicity of the new command, "Love one another.") Jesus is not pleased with Peter's deflection, and tells Peter he will soon deny him three times.

Failure as a disciple is what happens when we move from the central message of the new commandment. Jesus has told us what he wants: to love one another; to love as he loved.

The Father's House

During my almost forty years as pastor of Zebulon Baptist Church, many times I have stood in our pulpit and read these familiar words to a grieving family, congregation, and community:

> Do not let your hearts be troubled. You believe in God; believe also in me. My Father's house has many rooms; if that were not so, would I have told you that I am going there to prepare a place for you? And if I go and prepare a place for you, I will come back and take you to be with me that you also may be where I am. You know the way to the place where I am going. (John 14:1-4)

One could argue that in this text Jesus is telling his disciples he must leave them to go and be with God. He is promising them he will return and take them to the Father's house. We could assert this is much more about the promise of his return to earth than it is about heaven, a word not used in the text. Yet, I believe that Jesus intends these words to bring comfort to us in both life and death.

Out of love for his disciples Jesus brings up the whole idea of their continuing relationship even after he has left them. He does not want them to be anxious or troubled. He knows they believe in God; he asks them to trust him as well. In a short period of time—an amazing time that would include his death, burial, resurrection, and ascension—Jesus will no longer be with these beloved followers. But their relationship is not coming to an end. He is going to prepare a place for them in the Father's house and will come back to see them to that home. They will be together again. They simply need to trust him.

Of course, Thomas is confused. He does not know the way. How can such a promise be fulfilled? "I am the way and the truth and the life. No one comes to the Father except through me. If you really know me, you will know my Father as well. From now on, you do know him and have seen him" (John 14:6-7). Philip is curious about the idea that they now have seen and know the Father. Jesus lets Philip know that he is one with the Father; to have seen Jesus is to have seen the Father. And, Jesus promises that when he goes to the Father, "Very truly I tell you, whoever believes in me will do the works I have been doing, and they will do even greater things than these, because I am going to the Father. And I will do whatever you ask in my name, so that the Father may be glorified in the Son" (vv. 12-13). The conversation has pivoted away from comforting words about dwelling with Jesus in the Father's house.

I grew up in Atlanta, in the midst of the Bible Belt. The question of where one would spend eternity was *the* question. Being sure that you had taken care of a proper confession of faith in Jesus to assure you of heaven when you die was the central theme of the evangelical preaching I heard. It was the weekly focus of the time of invitation. Assent to the gospel's truth was one's passage to heaven. Failure to confess faith doomed one to hell for eternity. Nothing else rose to this level of importance. The anxious passion of the church longed for the salvation of souls.

It was quite a revelation after many years in ministry when I realized that Jesus never sounded an invitation anything like the ones that were so common in my upbringing. There was never a promise of heaven to a person willing to give assent to any propositional truths. Instead Jesus invited persons to follow, to become disciples, to live distinctly different from the kingdoms of the world and to live in and for the kingdom of God. Salvation is offered in the here and now; it is near, not far off. It is a journey of faithfulness to the call to follow.

But does this mean that the Christian hope of resurrection is unfounded? Did Jesus ignore our yearning to believe that even death does not separate us from God's love? No. Jesus wanted us to trust him. He wanted to calm restless, troubled hearts. "There are rooms in God's house. I am going to prepare your place. I will come again for you. Where I am, there with the Father, that is where you will be. I am the way to that place. Trust me."

My mother died of cancer at the young age of fifty-nine. She lived with our family near the end of her life, for my Dad had died of cancer several years earlier when he was fifty-three. On the last trip to a treatment in Raleigh before she would enter the hospital until her death, she asked me to be honest with her. "You are my son and now my pastor. I know you have studied and discussed these things. Do you really believe there is life after we die? Do you really believe I will go to heaven? Do you believe your dad is there? I don't want you to give me some pat answer. I want you to be honest with me. What do you believe?"

I am not sure I have ever had a more important conversation. I was quiet for a moment, careful to speak from a place of transparency and integrity. Eventually I said, "Mama, I can't prove anything to you. I wish I could, but I can't. Honestly, I don't trust the preachers who talk about heaven as a fact that cannot be questioned. But down deep in my soul or my gut I either believe or I don't. I either believe it all ends when we die or I believe we are somehow alive with God when we die. And, I really do believe it. It is a matter of trust. Jesus said there is a place for us. Jesus said he will take us to that place and we will continue to be together in that place he called the Father's house. I am trusting Jesus enough to hold on to faith and to hope and to love. Yes, down deep within me, I believe Dad is with God. I believe you will be soon. I don't know how it all works or exactly what it will be like, but yes, I believe you will be with Jesus."

My mother was quiet. She thought for a minute and then said, "You are a good son and pastor. I like your answer." She lived the remainder of her life with courage and strong faith. She followed Jesus with all she could. Her nurses fell in love with her. She encouraged them and listened to them and prayed with them. And then the end came. I believe she went to God's house. I believe Jesus took her to that place. I trust Jesus.

Some people will focus on Jesus' words in John 14 and find in them proof that only professing Christians make their way to heaven. This idea says more than Jesus intended. Jesus simply said that he is the way to the Father. Many Christians actually refute these words by insisting it is our profession of faith that saves us, that our profession reserves our room in heaven. Jesus is clear: he is the way, the truth, and the life. Many Christians are so certain of their own understanding of what is necessary for salvation, I fear that they would correct even God if salvation is granted by means beyond their understanding. Believing that life in God's presence with the Father and the Son is the prerogative of God and only God, of Jesus and only Jesus, is to leave issues of judgment and grace to God and God alone. It is to trust Jesus. Isn't that what Jesus was asking the disciples to do? Having trusted him enough to follow him in life, they were asked to trust him enough regarding their eternal destiny.

A Jesus worldview on eternal matters is important, even necessary. Reducing Christian faith to praying the prayer, or walking the aisle, or being baptized in order to go to heaven while all others go to hell misses out on so much of the teaching of Jesus. Our views of salvation must be focused on following Jesus, on proclaiming and living the kingdom of God, on obeying Jesus' teaching and following his example. We need to gladly leave questions of judgment up to God. We need to trust that God will judge rightly.

Becoming a disciple of Jesus and following Jesus is the essence of being a Christian, far more than simple intellectual assent to assertions of who Jesus is or what Jesus has done. That Jesus would tell parables of judgment should not be ignored. Neither should we ignore statements that speak of God loving the whole cosmos and saving the cosmos in John 3 or identifying Jesus as "the Lamb of God, who takes away the sin of the world" (John 1:29). And, we do not have to abandon our trust that we are somehow to be raised with Christ to enjoy our place in God's house. There are many rooms there, and Jesus has made us a promise. That should be enough to ease troubled hearts.

The Demonstration of Obedient Love

Hear these words from John 14: "If you love me, keep my commands" (v. 15). "Whoever has my commands and keeps them is the one who loves me" (v. 21). "Anyone who loves me will obey my teaching" (v. 23). "Anyone who does not love me will not obey my teaching" (v. 24).

It would be hard to miss the point Jesus drives home in the upper room. Love for Jesus is not demonstrated through flowery speech, or well thought-out theology, or professions of allegiance. Love for Jesus is shown through obedience. The greatest commandment must be observed. God must be loved with all our heart, soul, mind, and strength. And we must love our neighbor as ourselves. We must keep the new commandment and love one another. We must hear the words of his preaching and teaching and be wise to build our lives on the firm foundation of obedience to Jesus.

Jesus promises the presence of the Spirit for the help and comfort of the disciples. He does not want them to be anxious and dismayed over his leaving. He wants to leave them with peace and with the promise of God's Spirit being present with them. Jesus shares with the disciples a picture of the relationship they can continue to have with him after he departs. It is the picture of a growing vine:

> I am the true vine, and my Father is the gardener. He cuts off every branch in me that bears no fruit, while every branch that does bear fruit he prunes so that it will be even more fruitful . . . As the Father has loved me, so I have loved you. Now remain in my love. If you keep my commands, you will remain in my love, just as I have kept my Father's commands and remain in his love. I have told you this so that my joy may be in you and that your joy may be complete. My command is this: Love each other as I have loved you. (John 15:1-3, 9-12)

Jesus envisions a community of disciples after he leaves the world that will live in an organic, vital relationship with God, pictured as a vine and branches that bear fruit. The fruit is the fruit of obedience to the commands of Jesus. The simplest and most essential of which is to love. "Greater love has no one than this: to lay down one's life for one's friends. You are my friends if you do what I command" (John 15:13-14). One more time he makes his goal for them clear. "This is my command: Love each other" (v. 17).

A Jesus worldview sees the church as a community of Jesus-loving, Jesus-obeying followers who will love humanity as Jesus loved the human family. They will know his voice and obey it. Their love will know no boundaries. As friends of Jesus, they will love like Jesus loved. The fruit of their love will extend into all the earth. Their obedient love will bear the fruit of God's kingdom of heaven breaking in to the earth.

Obedient love will not be easy. There will be opposition to a community of Jesus followers committed to show their love for him by fully obeying his command to love. "If the world hates you, keep in mind that it hated me first" (John 15:18). Christ's suffering and sacrifice on the cross have meaning. Obedience to the teachings of Jesus is not unrelated to the atonement of Jesus. The very shape of his love for us is outlined by the cross. The consequence of his life of obedience to the Father marked by his radical, servant love was crucifixion. The world and its cultures are not cultures of love. Those religious and governmental cultures clashed with Jesus and insisted on his death. The more the church loves as Jesus commands, the more we will experience our own clashing with culture. The kingdoms of this world never make love a priority; the kingdom of God always makes love a priority.

It is possible to distort the teachings of Jesus and Scripture and turn Christian faith into something far different than Jesus envisioned. Distorted faith can make friends with culture, defending inequalities and injustice and excusing refusals to truly love. Authentic faith, obedient faith can never do that. We must call into question all that is unloving. That is what Jesus did—and what kept him in trouble. We are called to follow his example and obey his command. We are to love.

Over the years of ministry, I have received a lot of kind affirmations and a few criticisms, some well deserved, some not so much. Some of the affirmations and criticisms I should have just let go. Some of them I should have taken more to heart. But not long ago something offered as criticism became one of my most treasured affirmations.

Someone who has been subjected to listening to my preaching and teaching for too long (especially in his eyes) offered this critique. He said with seriousness, but not with any anger or malice: "The problem with you, Jack, is you are always preaching and teaching about love. Love, love, love. We need to hear more about judgment. We need to hear you preach against sins. Being a Christian is a whole lot more than just loving everybody."

I made sure I appeared at least somewhat chastised. But I would love to have kissed him and said a hearty, "Thank you!" The idea that my biggest error has been to emphasize love is a compliment to treasure. In truth, I know that I do not deserve such high praise. But I emphasize love because I am a follower of the one who said repeatedly in the upper room, "Love."

The Gift of the Spirit

John tells us that in the upper room, Jesus promises the disciples they will not be abandoned with his departure. They will receive the gift of the Spirit, the Advocate. The Spirit is sent from the Father just as the Son is sent from the Father. The Spirit will continue to "testify about me," Jesus tells his followers (15:26).

We need to recognize and embrace the continuing revelation of Christ through the work of the Spirit. One of the most neglected sayings of Jesus can be found in this discourse:

I have much more to say to you, more than you can now bear. But when he, the Spirit of truth, comes, he will guide you into all the truth. He will not speak on his own; he will speak only what he hears, and he will tell you what is yet to come. He will glorify me because it is from me that he will receive what he will make known to you. All that belongs to the Father is mine. That is why I said the Spirit will receive from me what he will make known to you. (John 16:12-15)

I have seldom heard any mention, much less emphasis, on the ongoing revelation of Jesus communicated through the Spirit. Jesus is clear: his teaching of his followers is unfinished. There was not time to say all he wanted to say. The time was not right to say some things he wanted to say. But the disciples are not to despair. At the right time the Spirit will continue to reveal truth from God to those who follow Jesus.

In his ministry Jesus helped his followers hear and see things in a different way. The Sermon on the Mount is filled with a section of discourse using the formula, "You have heard that it was said, but I say." Jesus interpreted scripture in a new light. He did not refute it but revealed a deeper meaning and understanding to what it truly meant to fulfill God's intent in those Scriptures. Now, from the upper room, Jesus says that this continuing revelation will take place, mediated by the Spirit.

In writing this work and quoting from the Gospels, I have noticed that my use of masculine pronouns for God has been so much greater than in my normal speech and teaching. That is because I am quoting the first-century gospel writers. Could it be that my heightened awareness of and sensitivity to gender issues could be the work of the Spirit, communicating truth from Jesus to me in the twenty-first century? Was this how the first-century church, led by Paul and to a lesser extent Peter, eventually moved beyond the insistence of the Judaizers to demand conformity to the law from Gentile Christians? Was Jesus teaching through the Spirit? Is this how Christians could come to see slavery and later racism in a true light, no longer finding proof texts from the Bible to defend these wrong practices, but exposing slavery and racism as truly evil? Was Jesus teaching those willing to be true disciples to listen to the Spirit? As many Christians are hearing Scripture differently and feeling called to give acceptance and affirmation to LGBTQ persons, could this be the right time for Jesus to continue to teach us, communicating new truth through the Spirit?

I can guess that this idea of Jesus giving the church new insights through the Spirit conjures up images of an unhealthy "slippery slope" for many people. I understand this concern. It seems to me that there are two points of view that followers of Jesus should avoid. One is to ignore this promise of Jesus to continue revealing new truth through the Spirit, choosing instead to defend traditional understanding of morals and values and treating Scripture as a closed book rather than believing "For the word of God is alive and active. Sharper than any double-edged sword, it penetrates even to dividing soul and spirit, joints and marrow; it judges the thoughts and attitudes of the heart" (Heb. 4:12). The scriptural interpretation of many Christians leaves no room for seeing Scripture in a new light. Thus, they perpetually defend the status quo with pious certainty that they are arguing for God and God's word. In reality, they are ignoring the promise of Jesus to continue to shed new light through the Spirit as new truth is communicated to his disciples.

There is a second problem to avoid: being too quick to dismiss the counsel of Scripture altogether and instead to adopt a position that "just seems right." Not every claim of conformity to the teaching of Jesus is accurate; not every new way of seeing comes from the Spirit. Jesus promising to continue to teach his followers through the Spirit's ongoing ministry is nothing at all like a blank check for everyone to do what seems right in their own eyes.

In the upper room, Jesus is speaking to the circle of disciples, the community he has created with them. There is more for them to learn. There is so much more he wants them to know, at the right time, when they are ready to see and hear in a new way. The Spirit can make this happen. Jesus will continue to be their trusted rabbi, their teacher in the faith.

It seems that a congregation, a fellowship of Jesus followers, should embrace this idea. We should hold fast to the preaching and study of inspired Scriptures through which God has spoken and continues to speak. But we should also be open to the new insights of Jesus as we seek to be authentic followers. The Spirit is at work in our midst if we are open. Healthy churches and healthy Christians embrace the continuing teaching ministry of Jesus in the Spirit. They practice discernment in community, holding on to God's truth but always in the fresh and renewing perspective of the Spirit. This is how Jesus believed his followers could change the world.

The gift of the Spirit will be the comfort and encouragement Christ's disciples need. His coming death, resurrection, and ascension will scatter them and challenge them. But Jesus wants them to find in the Spirit a holy boldness: Ask, and it will be granted. You will do great things in my name. Follow my example and obey my commandments and trust the work of the Spirit in you, for you, and in the world.

> But very truly I tell you, it is for your good that I am going away. Unless I go away, the Advocate will not come to you; but if I go, I will send him to you. When he comes, he will prove the world to be in the wrong about sin and righteousness and judgment: about sin, because people do not believe in me, about righteousness, because I am going to the Father, where you can see me no longer; and about judgment, because the prince of this world now stands condemned. (John 16:7-10)

Listen to Jesus: the world gets it wrong about sin, righteousness, and judgment. The Spirit is God's way of exposing how the world gets these things wrong, teaching the followers of Jesus. The world gets things wrong about sin because the world rejects Jesus' understanding of what is most important to God and what really constitutes rebellion against God. The world prefers traditional morality to the perspective Jesus offers.

Even after Jesus' ministry on earth is done, the work of exposing and correcting will continue in the Spirit. Jesus has told the disciples all of this for their benefit. "I have told you these things, so that in me you may have peace. In this world you will have trouble. But take heart! I have overcome the world" (John 16:33).

The Prayer of Jesus

The long discourse in John concludes with a beautiful prayer. Jesus is ready to face impending suffering leading to death. He prays:

> Father, the hour has come. Glorify your Son, that your Son may glorify you. For you granted him authority over all people that he might give eternal life to all those you have given him. Now this is

eternal life; that they know you, the only true God and Jesus Christ, whom you have sent. I have brought you glory on earth by finishing the work you gave me to do. (17:1-5)

The importance of the sacrifice of Jesus is not to be diminished by those who wish to live with a Jesus worldview. Yes, his teachings must shape that worldview. But his sacrifice is the crucial moment in time when the depth of God's love for the human family and plan for redemption and salvation is made clear. The universal implications of the death of Jesus should not be ignored, for clearly in this prayer God has given Jesus authority over all people, and now Jesus is preparing to give eternal life to all those the Father has given him. This gift of eternal life is to truly know God through the one who was sent, Jesus Christ.

Jesus prays for the disciples. Knowing that they will remain in the world, he asks, "Holy Father, protect them by the power of your name, the name you gave me, so that they may be one, as we are one" (John 17:11). Jesus asks for their protection against the evil one and that they may find within themselves a deep reservoir of joy—his joy. As they go into the world, he prays for their sanctification.

Jesus widens his prayer beyond the disciples to include all who have believed in him. He prays for the women and men who have dared to believe and follow, that they may be one with God and with one another. "I have given them the glory that you gave me, that they may be one as we are one— I in them and you in me—so that they may be brought to complete unity. Then the world will know that you sent me and have loved them even as you love me" (John 17:22-23).

Christ's large vision is for the world to know the love and goodness of God. His mission is to share that love with those who would believe, obey, and follow. A world living in union with God, one with God and one with one another, a union built on God's perfect love, is his goal. He wants that union to be lasting: "Father, I want those you have given me to be where I am, and to see my glory, the glory you have given me because you loved me before the creation of the world" (John 17:24). Jesus is willing to die for the world to know what it does not yet know: the deep love of God. His mission is to see God's love in us through him.

The Other Gospels

Matthew, Mark, and Luke also record remembrances from the upper room and Gethsemane. Their accounts are more succinct that John's, however. They give some detail of the betrayal to be carried out by Judas and of the predicted denial by Peter. Most important, these gospels tell us how Jesus took bread and wine and the words he said in sharing the bread and cup that have become the church's continual remembrance we call the Lord's Supper. Breaking the bread and sharing it with his disciples, Jesus said, "This is my body given for you; do this in remembrance of me" (Luke 22:19). Of the cup he said, "This cup is the new covenant in my blood, which is poured out for you" (v. 20).

The visual images of bread as his broken body and wine as his shed blood are powerful. Through the ages these images have shaped the faith of followers of Jesus as the church celebrates the Supper. At the center of Christian faith stands one who gave his body to be broken and gave his blood to be shed as an act of love, an act of loving obedience to the Father, an act of redeeming love for the world. Jesus shared that he would never eat the Passover feast again until its ultimate celebration when the kingdom of God is fulfilled.

Hopeful anticipation of that coming time when the kingdom is fully realized and we shall feast again with Jesus transforms the Supper into more than looking back to remember; it is also hopeful anticipation of a day that is yet to come. The blessing and breaking of the bread to eat and the blessing and sharing of the wine to drink help to shape the church's understanding of the Jesus it has promised to follow.

Questions for Discussion/Reflection

1. How well do you believe Christians uphold the model of foot washing for ministry? Do we practice a foot-washing style of servant leadership? What ministries in your church fellowship and to your community would honor the "foot washing" style of Jesus today?

2. Do you believe the new commandment to "love one another" is truly the central message to followers of Jesus? How well are we doing obeying this new commandment?

3. Do you see evidence of the world and culture resisting the central message that we are to love one another?

4. Articulate what you believe to be a healthy, Jesus-inspired understanding of life beyond this world. What role does the hope of being with God forever play in your own faith journey? How have you seen the message of the after-life actually be distorted by some Christians in ways that do not resonate with the teachings of Jesus?

5. Do you agree that love for Jesus is best demonstrated by obedience to his commands? Which teachings of Jesus seem hardest for you to keep? Where does the church seem to have the greatest struggle keeping Jesus' commands?

6. How did you react to the idea expressed in this chapter regarding the continuing teaching ministry of Jesus through the Spirit? What possible "red flags" did this raise for you? Do you think we have often been unwilling to accept the legitimate work of the Spirit to teach us new things that come from Jesus? Are there ways you see the Spirit actively teaching us and leading us today that come from the heart of Christ?

7. What captures your attention from the prayer Jesus offered for his disciples and others who believe?

8. How does the remembrance that takes place in the celebration of the Lord's Supper inform and shape your worldview?

CHAPTER 6

Seeing in the Passion and Resurrection

This final chapter looks at the narratives that detail the passion of Jesus and tell the stories of the risen Jesus. The death, burial, and resurrection narratives are central to Christian faith. Through the atoning work of Jesus on the cross and through Jesus being raised from the dead, we clearly see Jesus as the Son sent to earth, the gift of God's great love. Appropriating the cross and resurrection to our faith is a major theme in the Epistles of the New Testament, particularly in the writings of Paul. But the passion and resurrection narratives in the Gospels provide more than just theological argument for our Christian faith. They also help us construct a Jesus-centered worldview.

The Garden of Gethsemane

From the upper room Jesus walks with his disciples to Gethsemane. There he encourages them to pray. He moves further along with James, John, and Peter for his own time of prayer. The stress of the moment weighs heavily on Jesus: "My soul is overwhelmed with sorrow to the point of death" (Mark 14:34). Luke describes the intensity of the moment, writing, "And being in anguish, he prayed more earnestly, and his sweat was like drops of blood falling to the ground" (22:44).

Jesus' prayer is one of honest petition accompanied by obedient submission. "Father, if you are willing, take this cup from me; yet not my will, but yours be done" (Luke 22:42). Sadly, weary disciples are not able to share in this time of prayer, for Jesus finds them sleeping. That this vigil in the garden is largely unshared adds to the pathos of the moment. Jesus is agonizingly aware of the suffering immediately before him. He is willing to ask for relief from the Father, to be spared the bitter cup of sacrifice from which he is expected to drink. But ultimately Jesus is willing to submit to the suffering of the cross in anticipation of what the demonstration of love and mercy will do in reconciling God and humankind. His completely normal desire to be spared suffering is overcome by a greater desire, a desire to do what is intended to bring about redemption and salvation. He will submit to the will of God.

These narratives remind us of the true humanity of Jesus. The suffering of the cross is not an appearance of suffering; it is true suffering. His oneness with the Father and Spirit does not lessen the severity of his passion. The pain is enormous, the stress of the moment unbearable. But a larger motivation of love wins out. Jesus will keep on loving to the end. He willingly will pay an unimaginable price of great sacrifice.

My experience as a Christian in America struggles to grasp the enormity of this ordeal. But there are Christians, throughout history and in other places in the world today, who understand this struggle in ways far different from my own capacity to understand. Comparing any sacrifices I have made in following Jesus and any resistance I have encountered to the sacrifice of Jesus is impossible. It has cost me very little. But there have been and are martyrs for the faith.

Some people suffer physical harm, emotional distress, broken relationships, imprisonment, and the risk of death, but they continue to resolutely follow Jesus. Surely their resolve comes from the knowledge of the willingness of Jesus to suffer for us. They find strength and comfort in the knowledge that they are walking a difficult and lonesome path that Jesus walked for them long ago. Part of a Jesus worldview must speak to this sacrifice of Christ and how it relates to the suffering and sacrifice of Christians in various times and places.

Hearing American Christians today bemoan the attacks on Christianity and how they consider themselves a persecuted lot rings hollow. God must surely find us most ungrateful for the religious freedom we enjoy yet take for granted and are increasingly willing to deny to others who do not share our same faith perspectives. Suffering in Jesus' name is real, and it does happen. Gethsemane points us to prayer in those moments of trial. Like Jesus, the persecuted and martyred find their resolve in desiring something so much that they will not be deterred by suffering. That something is to please God, to follow Jesus.

With a Jesus worldview, we will avoid complaining about minor slights and inconveniences Christians may experience and resist a sense of entitlement that gives Christians favored status over others. This is not the way of Jesus. We will, however, be willing to put our lives on the line for Christ when the situation demands it. Like Jesus, Christians find strength in their own Gethsemane moments.

At Gethsemane, Jesus is betrayed and arrested. But he shows no anger toward his betrayer, Judas. He must do what he has come to do. Only a comment regarding the irony of betrayal with a kiss is sent his way. Jesus is surprised at the number of armed people sent to arrest him. How little they know about him if they sense he will fight against them. "Am I leading a rebellion," Jesus asks, 'that you have come out with swords and clubs to capture me? Every day I was with you, teaching in the temple courts, and you did not arrest me. But the Scriptures must be fulfilled" (Mark 14:48-49).

Submitting to the overreaching arm of unjust authority without resistance has become a model for the persecuted to follow. Conforming to scriptural depiction of the Suffering Servant in Isaiah 53, throughout the passion narratives we find Jesus quiet and submissive, yet strong and resolute. His reaction to arrest sets the stage for the rest of the story. Jesus keeps his wits about him and responds with neither angry, violent resistance nor with fear and cowardice. In his prayers at Gethsemane, Jesus has found strength to endure. His example has surely encouraged and inspired the persecuted through the ages. In Christ the prophets and crusaders for justice and righteousness find an example of how to endure suffering and persecution.

At the time of Jesus' arrest, some in the crowd of followers are ready to fight back. A companion draws his sword and cuts off the ear of one in the arresting party, but Jesus says to him: "Put your sword back in its place, for all who draw the sword will die by the sword. Do you think I cannot call on my Father, and he will at once put at my disposal more than twelve legions of angels?" (Matt. 26:52-53). The details in the Gospels of this incident vary a bit. One identifies the companion as Peter. The injured man is identified as a servant of the high priest. Luke tells us that Jesus heals the ear of the wounded man. But all four gospels agree in the nonviolent response of Jesus to a violent group sent to arrest him. At Gethsemane we encounter the peacemaking way of Jesus. There is no willingness to resort to violence in him.

Christians have chosen both pacifism and just-war theories in attempting to follow Jesus. Sadly, some will support almost any warlike effort of their nation and baptize it with Christian endorsement. No one can seriously argue that unbridled nationalism and militarism are consistent with a Jesus worldview. Some people will excuse Christian-endorsed militarism by pointing to the fact that Jesus acknowledged that there will be wars and rumors of wars in history and that even his own coming will not bring peace to every family, community, and nation. There are Christians who, in good conscience, can justify war only when it is motivated by love for the safety and freedom of others. Engaging in war to defend persons against violent, unwarranted aggression is reasonable. I tend to justify any engagement in war only for those very reasons. But a Jesus worldview that embraces complete pacifism is also reasonable. To follow the one who told his own disciples to put up their swords by adopting a nonviolent, peacemaking worldview makes sense.

The Trial

The trial of Jesus begins in front of Caiaphas, the high priest, and the Sanhedrin. It includes a procession of false witnesses, all willing to assist the elders and teachers of the law with their intent to find compelling evidence that will lead to Jesus' death.

Throughout the testimony of these false witnesses Jesus remains silent. Finally, the high priest is ready to cut to the chase, asking Jesus, "I charge you under oath by the living God: Tell us if you are Messiah, the Son of God." Jesus replies, "You have said so. But I say to all of you: From now on you will see the Son of Man sitting at the right hand of the Mighty One and coming on the clouds of heaven." Then the high priest tears his clothes and claims, "He has spoken blasphemy! Why do we need any more witnesses? Look, now you have heard the blasphemy. What do you think?" The witnesses answer, "He is worthy of death" (Matt. 26:63-66).

The dramatic rending of Jesus' garments by Caiaphas reveals what the spiritual leaders of Judaea cannot tolerate about Jesus. They cannot accept any claims by Jesus or his followers that he is the Son of God, the Messiah. One might question how open these men would be to the coming of any messiah. But they definitely are not open to embrace the possibility that a poor man from Galilee with his unimpressive band of followers could be the Messiah. Jesus could certainly capture the interest of multitudes with his wondrous works and insightful teaching. But the Messiah that the religious leaders expected would come to restore the fortunes of the nation, a new David, charismatic and appealing. Jesus did not fit their understanding of the promised anointed one. Therefore, convinced that he is no messiah, any claims to the contrary are considered blasphemous. The anger of these elders of Israel toward Jesus lead them to hit him, spit at him, and mock him.

As we consider the idea of a Jesus worldview, this reticence before his accusers is worth noting. Ultimately, Caiaphas is right about at least one thing: the crux of the matter is the consideration that Jesus is the anointed one of God, God's Son, the Christ, the Messiah. If Jesus is none of those things, then his own admissions and the claims of his followers really do not constitute blasphemy. But persons of faith do see Jesus as the Son of God. We view Jesus as the Christ. We confess faith that hails Jesus as Lord and Savior.

How could the elders of Israel miss who Jesus really was? The main reason is that he did not come in ways they expected the Messiah would come. The humility of Jesus, the vulnerability of Jesus, and the failure of Jesus to confront Israel's enemies and to restore the fortunes of God's people all caused these elders to question his claims and to reject him altogether.

The reality is that Jesus conformed to a very different image of the Messiah. Jesus took on the role of a suffering servant, certainly an idea expressed in the Old Testament, particularly in the latter portions of Isaiah. But the messianic hopes of Israel did not rest on one who would come to suffer in humility, but on one who would come to rule in glory. Jesus resisted more militant and more glorious patterns to shape his life and ministry and instead embraced the pattern of the obedient servant willing to suffer for the sake of others.

Christians read the stories of Christ's passion, particularly his submissive spirit and reluctance to offer a saving defense for himself, and quickly recognize great correlation to passages of Scripture in Isaiah that describe one who "was pierced for our transgressions" (53:5) and "was oppressed and afflicted, yet he did not open his mouth" (v. 7). This is not to say that these passages are simply a foretelling of the sacrifice of Jesus; that does injustice to authentic Hebrew interpretation of these Scriptures. The most likely interpretation of this passage is to view Israel as the true suffering servant. The passage gives ultimate redemptive meaning to the long struggles and suffering of Israel.

Most significantly, Jesus, who was well versed in the Scriptures and quite aware of the expectations of Israel for the Son of God and Messiah, conformed himself to the image of the suffering servant. In the trial we see a submission to his fate of suffering that is not a sign of weakness or resignation, but a strong willingness to lay down his life for others. Jesus had said before his arrest and trial, "The reason my Father loves me is that I lay down my life—only to take it up again. No one takes it from me, but I lay it down of my own accord. I have authority to lay it down and authority to take it up again" (John 10:17-18).

There are two implications here for followers of Jesus. First, we realize that Christians have staked their faith in the idea that Jesus is God's Son, God's anointed one. Jesus is both Lord and Christ to the church. Second, we must take seriously what Jesus models in the trial and subsequent suffering: The one who is truly of God suffers for the sake of others.

The world sees greatness in a different light. Greatness is associated with power and popularity. Greatness is measured by success, often material success. Attractive traits and qualities accompany greatness. Jesus rejected these cultural notions of greatness. Great love, great obedience, and great sacrifice—these are the virtues Jesus taught, and in the passion narratives, these are now the virtues Jesus exhibits, no matter what the cost to himself.

The trial shifts to the Roman governor, Pilate. The elders want Jesus killed, and they want this done by the Romans. Pilate has no concern for issues of blasphemy. Therefore, they tell Pilate that Jesus claims to be a king; his inciting the crowds could be viewed as insurrection, a crime against Caesar and worthy of death. Pilate asks Jesus, "Are you the king of the Jews?" Jesus replies, "You have said so" (Luke 23:3). Pilate then tells the chief priests he finds no fault in Jesus. But they insist he is a threat to Rome because of his potential to stir the crowds.

Pilate is amazed that Jesus hears the accusation without responding, without fighting back. Eventually, with reluctance, Pilate will offer either Jesus or Barabbas for release at Passover. The crowd can choose between the notoriously violent Barabbas or Jesus. They choose Barabbas and call for the execution of Jesus. After a painful beating and more mockery and physical abuse from the Roman soldiers, the cross awaits.

The Cross

On the way to the cross, Jesus sees people following and women who are mourning and wailing for him. He tries to comfort them: "Daughters of Jerusalem, do not weep for me; weep for yourselves and for your children" (Luke 23:28). Reaching Golgotha, the place of his execution, Jesus is nailed to a cross and hung with criminals on either side. The long and torturous execution by crucifixion begins. The crowd of witnesses include those who continue to mock and insult Jesus, along with a few women who love him and at least one disciple.

Our remembrance of the crucifixion is punctuated by the seven sayings from the cross recorded in the Gospels. The first is a word of forgiveness: "Father, forgive them, for they do not know what they are doing" (Luke 23:34). The second is a word of grace extended to one of the dying men beside him. This man has asked, "Jesus, remember me when you come into your kingdom" (v. 42). Jesus answers, "Truly I tell you, today you will be with me in paradise" (v. 43). When Jesus sees Mary, his mother, standing with three other women and John ("the disciple whom he loved") at the cross, he says to her: "Woman, here is your son," and to the disciple, "Here is your mother." From that time on, the disciple takes Mary into his care (John 19:26-27).

In the first three sayings from the cross we encounter the amazing capacity of Jesus to focus on the needs of others before his own. The one who taught us to love our enemies and to forgive repeatedly finds the grace and compassion within himself to plead to the Father that the sins of his tormentors and executioners be forgiven. A person deserving of punishment turns to him and receives compassionate words of promise and assurance. The man will be with Jesus this very day in paradise. His love for Mary is never more apparent than in this recognition of his mother from the cross and his concern for her future well-being.

So many of the teachings of Jesus related to love, sacrifice, service, and forgiveness seem to be impossible to fully put into practice. Yet, from the agony, embarrassment, and suffering of the cross Jesus is practicing exactly what he has preached. He is full of grace and mercy, love and compassion. At the cross we see that the values of love and compassion are to be lived out in any and every circumstance of life. At the cross we see what the hymn writer Isaac Watts expressed so eloquently, "Love so amazing, so divine, demands my soul, my life, my all."

Both the physical pain and spiritual/emotional pain of the cross are reflected in the next two statements from the cross. The admission, "I am thirsty" (John 19:28), leads to the extension of a vinegar-soaked sponge to touch his lips. As the day progresses, about three in the afternoon, Jesus cries in agony, "*Eli, Eli, lema sabachthani?*—"My God, my God, why have you forsaken me?" (Matt. 27:46).

Thy mystery of incarnation invites us to hold to the dual truths that Jesus is both fully God and fully human. At the crucifixion Jesus does not just appear human, but is indeed human. The torturous means of execution is excruciatingly painful. The suffering of Christ is indeed real. The emotional toll of it all leads to the moment when he cries out to God with a cry of abandonment. Indeed, Jesus empties himself completely on the cross, even to the place where he feels forsaken by the Father with whom at all other times he has experienced a deep union, a oneness.

A Jesus worldview shaped by the cross takes pain and suffering seriously. But it also embraces suffering when it is necessary for a greater good. The price the cross exacts from Jesus—physically, spiritually, and emotionally—is enormous. But Jesus pays the price. He endures the cross for a greater outcome, a deeper joy that can only become possible through his sacrifice. Finally, the suffering nears the end and Jesus offers, "It is finished" (John 19:30). He cries out with a loud voice, "Father, into your hands I commit my spirit" and then breathes his last breath (Luke 23:46).

The gospel writers recount the awesome drama of that particular moment: "The curtain of the temple was torn into from top to bottom. And when the centurion, who stood there in front of Jesus, saw how he died, he said, 'Surely this man was the Son of God!'" (Mark 15:38-39). "The earth shook, the rocks split and the tombs broke open. The bodies of many holy people who had died were raised to life" (Matt. 27:51-52). The barrier of the temple veil breaks; in his sacrifice Jesus has made access to the very presence of a holy God possible. A victory over death has been won by his sacrifice, thus tombs can be opened. And, a Roman centurion can now see what the priests and elders of Israel could not see; surely Jesus must be the Son of God.

It is tempting to confine the worldview of Jesus to a survey of the essence of his teachings. But I believe that seeing with Jesus also includes a close look at the death of Jesus. At the heart of the Christian faith lies a great mystery, often recited in communion liturgy: "Christ has died. Christ has risen. Christ will come again." Seeing Jesus on the cross, to appreciate the enormity of his suffering and the inexhaustible capacity he had for both loving and forgiving, is an integral part of the development of a Jesus worldview. The powerful and central symbol of the cross for Christian faith properly shapes the thoughts and actions of anyone who takes seriously the call to follow Jesus. Jesus taught that discipleship involves taking up one's own cross. What that really means can only be understood and appreciated by first looking at the cross on which Jesus died. We must truly see how Jesus bore his cross before we can begin to start the journey of bearing our own crosses.

The Resurrection

The Gospel of Mark reports the visit to Jesus' grave by the women on the first day of the week, just after sunrise. They find the stone rolled away and the tomb of Jesus empty. A young man dressed in white is there to the right. The whole thing is frightening. "'Don't be alarmed,'" he tells the women. "You are looking for Jesus the Nazarene, who was crucified. He has risen! He is not here. See the place where they laid him. But go, tell his disciples and Peter'" (16:6-7).

The women hear the astounding news but cannot help but be alarmed. Trembling and bewildered, they flee from the tomb. They say nothing to anyone, because they are afraid (v. 8). The oldest manuscripts of Mark end here. While appreciative of the more traditional gospel texts we read for Resurrection Sunday, I also like this telling of the story.

Resurrection is fearful. When we visit cemeteries, we visit graves. We pay our respects. We cherish our memories. We express our grief. Open graves with some strange person's promise of resurrection would alarm us indeed. While I love to sing, "Alleluia! He is risen indeed" at Easter, I also like expressing resurrection in more dramatic terms: "Jesus is loose!" The realization that Jesus is loose from the grave and alive produces a certain fearful reverence that makes one a bit more careful about making Jesus pronouncements. Those who would articulate a worldview consistent with Jesus would do well to respect that Jesus is loose. As the wonderful George Burns film *Oh, God!* portrays beautifully, there are more than a few preachers who should take seriously their pronouncements regarding God's will and ways. If we really believed that Jesus might indeed appear, we might use far more caution in articulating a biblical or Christian worldview so different from a Jesus worldview.

Of course, there are two separate endings added to Mark. One has Jesus appearing to Mary Magdalene, who then reports the resurrection news to disbelieving disciples. Those disciples do not believe the reports of two others who claim to have encountered Jesus while on a walk in the country. Jesus appears, eventually, to the eleven, admonishing them for failing to believe the report of witnesses. He blesses them with a commissioning that includes their driving out demons, speaking in tongues, handling snakes, and drinking poison without harm—fearful stuff to ponder, indeed!

Luke tells a beautiful tale of Jesus coming alongside two pilgrims returning from Jerusalem after the Passover. They are on the way home to Emmaus. They are surprised that their new travel companion seems to know nothing of the news—news that Jesus of Nazareth was crucified and that some of the women who followed him are reporting his resurrection. He says to them, "How foolish you are, and how slow to believe all that the prophets have spoken! Did not the Messiah have to suffer these things and then enter his glory?" Then he explains to them what was said in the Scriptures concerning himself (24:25-27).

Jesus had persisted in telling his disciples that he must suffer and die, but he was just as persistent in telling them he would be raised to new life. Jesus trusted God's promise of resurrection. Not only did the disciples invariably argue with Jesus about the necessity of his suffering, but also after his death and early news of his overcoming the grave, they are just as slow to dare to embrace resurrection faith. These two travelers finally make it home and invite their mystery guest to enjoy dinner. In the breaking of bread, they realize their fellow traveler has been Jesus. Their eyes are opened to see him alive and in their midst.

John tells of the risen Jesus appearing in the midst of the disciples. The repeated greeting from the risen Christ to his disciples is "Peace be with you!" (John 20:19). His resurrection is to bring them shalom, contentment, peace. A doubting Thomas has to see for himself, just as the other ten have seen, the wounded side and hands of Jesus. The risen Lord is indeed Jesus, the crucified.

John also recounts a wonderful story of Jesus appearing to the disciples by the Sea of Galilee. Once again, they find Jesus capable of helping them bring in a huge haul of fish after a night with little luck. Grilling fish over charcoal for a breakfast with the disciples, Jesus confronts Peter. Three times Jesus asks Simon Peter if he, indeed, truly loves him. Peter answers with a "yes" each time, grieved that Jesus has to ask three times. But there are some interesting things going on in the Greek text that English translations easily miss in reporting this conversation.

Jesus asks the first two times if Peter loves him, using a form of the word, *agape,* for "love." This is a self-giving, sacrificial love. Surprisingly, Peter confesses a more humble form of love, *philo,* an affectionate love. By the third time Jesus asks if Peter loves him with this affectionate love, Peter vows, "Lord, you know all things; you know that I love you" (John 21:17). After three times asking Peter if he loves him and Peter saying that he does, Jesus instructs Peter to feed or take care of his sheep.

In this exchange Peter seems to have finally discovered a new honesty and humility in the presence of the risen Christ. Peter has learned through his own unfortunate denial of Jesus and through the death of Jesus on the cross that he can no longer claim a love for Jesus that matches or exceeds Jesus' love for him. Jesus knows Peter loves him, but certainly with an imperfect, sometimes faltering love. Jesus accepts that love. All that he asks is for Peter to love others for him; to take care of, lead, and tend all of his sheep and lambs.

Matthew's gospel ends with a beloved commission of the disciples by the risen Jesus: "All authority in heaven and on earth has been given to me. Therefore, go and make disciples of all nations, baptizing them in the name of the Father and of the Son and of the Holy Spirit, and teaching them to obey everything that I have commanded you. And surely I am with you always, to the very end of the age" (Matt. 28:18-20).

Luke describes a similar commissioning at the time of Jesus' ascension in the first chapter of Acts, "But you will receive power when the Holy Spirit comes on you; and you will be my witnesses in Jerusalem, and in all Judea and Samaria, and to the ends of the earth" (Acts 1:8). In these words of commissioning Jesus encourages his disciples to carry out their divinely appointed mission. They are to be witness as they go, making disciples among all nations.

We need to see the call for continued disciple-making. Jesus is looking for more than adherents or admirers in the future; he wants women and men to follow him just as the first generation of disciples followed him. They are to go and share the gospel everywhere, close and far away, in the comfortable and not-so-comfortable places. The message is for everyone. Yes, Christ-followers are to invite new disciples to give witness to their faith through a baptism in the name of the Father, Son, and Holy Spirit. But there is a mission beyond evangelizing and baptizing new converts. They are to teach the new followers all that Jesus has taught them. Any presentation of Jesus that calls for a profession of faith and baptism without an emphasis on obedience to his teachings is incomplete.

Looking at the resurrection appearances together as recorded in the Gospels, we can see several issues relevant to a Jesus worldview. First, note the continued encouragement to "fear not" and the continuing offer from the risen Jesus, "Peace be with you." True followers of Jesus move from fear and anxiety to trust and confidence. They see the world from a place of peace, not a place of fear. Christian voices that seem consumed by fear and anxiety and who stir up those fears in others are inconsistent with the voice of the risen Christ.

The resurrection renewed the discipleship of the remaining eleven and other followers of Jesus. The resurrection keeps us moving forward in our own discipleship. Loved by the perfect love of Jesus who demonstrated that love in his passion, we love Jesus in return, with a less than perfect love, but with a genuine love, nonetheless. We show our love for Jesus by tending to and caring for those he loved, a wide flock of beloved sheep that excludes no one in the human family.

We encourage discipleship in others, and we celebrate their willingness to follow Christ in baptism. But even after baptism, the real work of being a follower remains. That work involves being taught all that Jesus taught, so that our character is shaped and our lives are directed by his teaching. The end goal of discipleship is obedience motivated by love, just as Jesus said, "If you love me, keep my commandments" (John 14:15).

Hopefully, this chapter has made a case for linking the passion narratives of Jesus with the teaching, disciple-making, and healing ministries of Jesus. That connection has too often been weak among Christians. We have focused on salvation through professing faith so that we can be assured of eternal salvation. Then after we become Christians, we seek to live obediently by studying the words of Scripture, including those found in the Gospels. But the emphasis is on professing faith more than on living faith. And, unfortunately, this reduces the definition of what it truly means to be a Christian to that of assenting to propositional truths about Jesus and with far less regard for a personal and communal commitment to follow Jesus. Too many people have been evangelized without discipleship. That makes the church quite vulnerable to false teachers who espouse as biblical or Christian those worldviews that are inconsistent with or dismissive of the teachings of Jesus.

At the same time, any Jesus worldview initiative that places almost all of the emphasis on the teachings of Jesus while reducing in any way the importance of the death, burial, and resurrection of Jesus is unfortunate. The church of this day and age must rise above a dichotomy in thinking that we either emphasize salvation by grace through faith or we emphasize discipleship that obeys the teaching of Jesus. We must do both! Like Paul, "I want to know Christ—yes, to know the power of his resurrection and participation in his sufferings, becoming like him in death, and so, somehow attaining to the resurrection from the dead" (Phil. 3:10-11).

Discipleship is not step two in the Christian life: it is the very essence of the Christian life. Discipleship begins with a willingness to trust the one who calls us to follow. It seeks to know Jesus in every way—to know his teaching and to know his sacrifice; to know his healing and to know his resurrection.

The goal of Christians and congregations in our context must be to know, love, and follow Jesus. A balanced understanding that finds the teaching of Jesus inseparable from the passion of Jesus is needed. His teaching was pointed toward the cross and resurrection; he tried to tell his disciples of its coming necessity time and time again. Jesus' death and resurrection validated his teaching and ministry and empowered his followers to remember his words and deeds and obey them, freed from fear, strengthened by his peace and by the presence of his Spirit. When we get this right, a holistic view of the Christian life of discipleship, we will both see Jesus and see with Jesus. This is truly my heartfelt and fervent prayer for my life and for the life of the church. Amen. Let this be!

Questions for Discussion/Reflection

1. What inspires you about the prayer Jesus offered in Gethsemane? How could the disciples have slept through such a moment? In what ways do you find Christians sleeping today when we need to be fully awake?

2. We certainly should be grateful for the religious freedom afforded us to worship and serve God as we choose. But this has made our following Jesus far easier than many people have experienced in the past and at other places

in the world today. Do you believe the relative ease of our practice of faith has hampered our discipleship? Has it perhaps contributed to the ease with which some people can distort, ignore, or avoid the teachings of Jesus to propose a Christian or biblical worldview radically different from that of Christ's? Without relinquishing religious freedom that we should cherish, how can we authentically make our discipleship more costly?

3. How do you view the example and teaching of Jesus with regard to violence? How can a Jesus worldview effectively address issues of violence and war in our current context?

4. How does the calm and quiet demeanor of Jesus during an unjust trial accompanied by mockery and assault affect you as a follower? What do you think Jesus was trying to show us and teach us by his handling of this ordeal?

5. What lessons did Jesus continue to teach from the cross? Which of those lessons proves the most difficult for you and/or your church to embrace?

6. How does the resurrection of Jesus help to shape your Jesus worldview?

7. How does resurrection faith empower the church? Does it truly increase peace and confidence while lowering fear and anxiety? Does much of what we hear today in the name of a biblical or Christian worldview increase or diminish anxiety and fear?

8. How do you think the commissioning of disciples by the risen Christ Jesus can best be lived out by Christians and congregations in the world today?

9. Should the teachings of Jesus be inseparably linked to the passion of Jesus? Why or why not? When have you seen these separated, and what effect did this cause? What examples have you seen of healthy integration of the passion of Jesus with his teachings?

EPILOGUE

As I finished writing the final chapter of this work and began to reflect on what I had written, it was easy to be critical. Looking over the six chapters, I recognized that for the most part I was simply quoting from the Gospels. Yes, there was a different way of organizing the stories and words of Jesus and there was a persistent effort to reflect on how these stories and words can help us view the world as Jesus viewed the world. But there was little more to see in this book other than the gospel accounts of the life and ministry of Jesus Christ.

My own critique can in one way be affirmation, however. The whole thesis behind this work is that many claims by Christians that they represent a Christian or biblical worldview are invalid. Their words sound little like the words of Jesus. Their points of emphasis are often ideas scarcely or never addressed by Jesus. The strong themes that emerge as priorities in the teaching of Jesus are not embraced in these supposed biblical and Christian worldviews. The persons promoting these worldviews are often prominent religious, media, and political personalities. In an age when biblical literacy is in decline, their claims to represent Christian thinking go largely unchallenged. In fact, their voices help to shape public opinion. The result is a culture with a significant number of professing Christians endorsing religious, social, media, and political leaders as authentic proponents of a Christian and biblical worldview, when in actuality these persons propose a worldview far different from that of Jesus. Sincere Christians and congregations embrace these worldviews as their own, lacking the confidence and/or knowledge to call these views into question.

The corrective for these false claims of Christian and biblical worldviews must be to reexamine the Gospels. We must look carefully at the life of Jesus as we know it from the gospel accounts. A Christian should desire to see the world as Jesus saw the world. What other way can we do that than to become devoted to his teachings, attentive to the way he lived, and accepting of the things he prioritized?

The need for Jesus-centered practice of Christian faith is tremendous in our day and age. Cultural Christianity is far more concerned with election outcomes and defending a prevalent cultural spirit of the age than with developing faithful followers of Jesus and Jesus-centered congregations. Arguments played out on social media between persons with differing worldviews will accomplish little. But a simple call to read the Gospels and honestly appropriate what we learn has the potential to accomplish much. Persons of goodwill who want to follow Jesus can surely agree that studying his life and teaching is a good thing. As we discuss the Gospels, we may yet have different interpretations of some of what Jesus said and did. Discussing the same texts, we may disagree over how Jesus saw the world. But Jesus was a plain speaker and a man of consistent action. Christians, congregations, and the larger Christian community have the capacity to center their thoughts and actions around the thoughts and actions of Jesus. A gospel-informed, Jesus-centered faith is both imminently possible and urgently needed.

The call to articulate for our day and age a Jesus worldview is significant. Declining participation and confidence in the church is a reality congregations and denominations have faced for several decades. The number of persons who view Christian religion as more detrimental to the betterment of society is dramatically rising. And, the voices of those insisting their worldviews are the true expressions of Christian faith are loud, intense, and often, coercive.

A different voice needs to be heard. A different way of living needs to be apparent. A new vision needs to take shape. That this emergence would come from Christians and congregations sincerely wanting to be true to Jesus would be marvelous. Jesus clearly taught that he was motivated by the inbreaking of the kingdom of God, a kingdom far different from all the other kingdoms of this world. Followers of Jesus should care little for using Christian faith to help attain power in our worldly, cultural kingdoms. Instead, we should model a life committed to following Jesus. We should declare a vision of the world consistent with the worldview of Jesus.

Is such a thing possible? I believe it is. I do not believe we ever get a Jesus worldview one hundred percent correct, nor do I believe we live like Jesus lived and as he wants us to live all of the time. But I do believe the desire to know the worldview of Jesus leads to knowledge and discernment, and the desire to be obedient to Jesus leads to a better way of living. I believe there are Christian communities that strive to sharpen their view of the world to be more consistent with a Jesus worldview, communities of mutual encouragement that prioritize fidelity with Jesus.

I have been blessed to serve one community of faith for more than forty years, to share life with a marvelous group of sisters and brothers in Christ. I would never suggest that we are a perfect, or even exceptional, community of faith. We are far too imperfect for such a claim. We don't always look like a Jesus-centered community should look, and we don't always say and do what a Jesus-centered community should say and do. But we do focus on knowing Jesus and following Jesus, however imperfectly. And, we do our best to swim upstream against the currents of cultural Christianity with their worldview so different from the worldview of Jesus.

We could all name persons of celebrity status who we believe embody a Jesus worldview. From my perspective, Mother Teresa and Martin Luther King Jr. embodied a Jesus worldview well. I believe my Jesus worldview has been shaped by Christian leaders and authors. Frederick Buechner and Henri Nouwen come to mind. The recent death of Rachel Held Evans caused me to grieve, although I had never met her. But her voice was an important voice; through her writings she helped me to sharpen my own view of the world as Jesus saw the world. Reading her blogs often felt like I was seeing with Jesus.

If a Jesus worldview movement is to gain momentum, however, I sense that it will come less from prominent leaders and more from faithful individuals and communities of faith. The desire to be more authentic in our living as followers of Jesus needs to be a true grassroots movement. Speakers and authors and leaders can be helpful, but only to the degree that they call us to be more Jesus-centered. My hope is that the Spirit might do just what Jesus promised, guiding us to faithful understanding and teaching us the things of Christ.

For those who might be close to losing heart that a credible witness to a Jesus worldview is even possible today, look around you. The disheartening reaction to those prominent voices speaking from their biblical and Christian worldviews in ways so incongruent with the teachings of Jesus can be countered. You *can* find faithful followers of Jesus. They *do* see the world remarkably like Jesus. They *are* shaped by his teaching, his ministry, and his passion. Following their lead and joining their ranks is the best contribution we can make to the advancement of an authentic Jesus worldview.

I see authentic glimpses of persons living consistently with an authentic Jesus worldview within my own faith community and in faithful congregations nearby. I see the hungry being fed. I see clothing provided to those who need it. I see forgiveness practiced and grace extended. I see genuine hospitality offered without boundaries and exceptions.

There is a woman in her mid-nineties in our congregation who I always hope visitors will sit near in worship, for if they do, they will be welcomed with exceptional warmth and genuine graciousness. I continue to see in her an openness to learn more about Jesus and a willingness to put what she learns into practice.

Another person who has been a part of my journey is Becky. She was widowed at an early age with two teenage sons. She bore her grief, loved her sons, and made it through the ordeal of becoming single again. She loved children, much like Jesus loved children. She played piano for our Cherub Choir. She worked with children in Vacation Bible School every year, usually in crafts. She offered to be a "Grandma" during worship for children of choir members. She would escort their children from their Sunday School classes to the sanctuary and sit with them so that their parents could lead in worship. My own two children sat with Becky for years.

When we built a new sanctuary, Becky made an unbelievable commitment. She had already signed her retirement papers to leave years of being a teacher's assistant in our elementary school. But with a new sanctuary under construction, she asked her principal if she could work for three more years. He was delighted. She gave all the difference between her calculated retirement income and earned income over the next three years to build the new sanctuary. Plus, money she had saved for a new heating system in her home she gave for the new place of worship. She was never happy that I knew any of this, but her son, a good friend and minister, shared this with me.

Becky was a faithful daughter. Her compassionate care of her mother and of an aunt who had no children was remarkable. Her ministry to elderly persons in our community was loving and consistent. She loved to carry tapes of the Sunday services to homebound members and to give them the gift of extended visits and interested listening.

Becky was a tremendous seamstress. Her great passion in the church was our clothes closet ministry. As persons brought in discarded clothing, Becky took the items home to prepare them for distribution. She washed and ironed the clothes and mended them if needed. Every garment that made it to our clothing racks was in good shape. And, twice a week, she headed up our crew of volunteers to open the clothes ministry. Becky treated each guest with warmth. Persons selecting clothes from our ministry were treated as if they were customers at a fashionable boutique. Becky's home-baked cookies were often there for everyone to enjoy. Becky insisted that other volunteers follow her lead; no one should be embarrassed by coming to the church for help, but all should be treated as welcomed guests.

Becky could be stern at times. She loved me and I certainly loved her. But there were times she let me know the church could and should do better. In each of those occasions I knew Becky was standing up for persons Jesus would stand up for and support—the poor, the needy, the broken, the children, the elderly.

Becky died years ago. But if I want to consider if living with a Jesus worldview is possible, she comes to mind. There are many others with amazing stories I could tell, many still living and active in our church and community. They inspire me to believe in the value of pursuing a Jesus worldview and living consistently with that worldview.

It is my hope that reading this book has given you a fresh look at the life and teaching of Jesus—his sermon on the mount, his relationship with the disciples, his encounters with others, his teaching, his discourse from the upper room, and his death and resurrection. Perhaps this book has contributed in some small way to a better understanding of how Jesus saw the world. And, hopefully this in turn increases your desire to see with Jesus and to let that vision direct your life. I can think of no better way to live.